MONEY TALKS

T0302796

MONEY TALKS

BRITISH MONARCHS AND HISTORY IN COINS

AN INTRODUCTION

BOB WHITTINGTON

IN ASSOCIATION WITH VITABIOTICS

Whittles Publishing

Published by
Whittles Publishing Ltd.,
Dunbeath,
Caithness, KW6 6EG,
Scotland, UK
www.whittlespublishing.com

© 2017 Bob Whittington

ISBN 978-184995-316-0

Production managed by Jellyfish Solutions Ltd

CONTENTS

ACKNOWLEDGEMENTS

I am very grateful to the following for their kind permission to reproduce the images of their coins:

David Powell – www.leadtokens.org.uk

Dix Noonan Webb

Parliamentary Archives, London

Royal Mint

Simon Hall – www.hallshammeredcoins.com

Trustees of the British Museum

INTRODUCTION

Ever since the first coin was struck from electrum (an alloy of gold and silver), probably around 600 BC in Asia Minor (present-day Turkey), we have been obsessed with money. Coins tell us about kings and queens; they mark the transfer of power, and they trace the relationships and influences of neighbouring countries between and on each other.

For collectors they are objects of beauty and value; in days gone by they would have been worn as adornments and jewellery. For our story they are the signposts along the way as ancient Britain struggled from being an island of independent warlike tribes, fighting for survival among themselves and from outside invaders bent on pillaging and conquering, to a nation which would eventually have imperial ambitions of her own. Monarchs have minted it and manipulated it, hoarded it and squandered it, but all have relied on money as they campaigned to acquire lands and establish their right to the throne. In modern times coinage has been used to mark special occasions rather than to signify and underline authority and power.

Coins are the tell-tale evidence throughout history of conquests and defeats, of power struggles and pride. They also mark changing attitudes and values – how we moved from bartering for goods to cash for everything, from buying bread to bribery.

Once they were rare, rough and ready, and had to be weighed to calculate value; today they are milled, engraved, and polished. In time we may do without coins altogether in our electronic and digital world, or we may even revert to bartering once again as some do today, trading what they have or can grow in exchange for items they desperately need but cannot afford to buy with money.

Money Talks traces British history through the one thing that has come to dominate our lives – hard cash. It looks at what was happening to the country as it emerged from its early history and royal struggles with cash flow problems to modern times, and sees what the thrymsa, the penny, and the groat have to tell us about those times and the people who used them.

It may now be decimalised, it may even move virtually at the swipe of an electronic card, but money has survived for more than 2,500 years, rising and falling in value, changing in shape and size, and merging into a continent-wide single unit. The coin will go on talking, telling its own unique tale about the lives we lead, the challenges we face, and the dreams we are trying to turn into reality.

1 IRON AGE – ROMAN BRITAIN

Hard as many Britons might find it as we rail against Europe and its perceived interference in our way of life, clinging proudly to our independence as an island nation while conveniently forgetting how often we have been invaded, the first coins we used were actually from what is now France. They were minted by a Celtic tribe in Belgica. The Belgae was a loose grouping of tribes with different ethnic origins – those in modern-day northern France were Celtic Gauls.

The period we refer to as the Iron Age stretches from 800 BC to as late as AD 100, well into the Romanisation of Britain; in Scotland, which the Romans tried and failed to conquer, it reaches into the fifth century AD. During this time the Celts were the dominant group in north-west Europe, eventually arriving in Britain around 100 BC.

To add insult to injury as we watched Greece stumble under the burden of impossible debt in the twenty-first century, that first coin was a copy of the beautiful gold stater of Phillip II of Macedonia (382–336 BC), father of Alexander the Great. Britain, although of course it only became a united country under that name by the Act of Union creating the United Kingdom of Great Britain in 1707, was a long way behind. Even when the first coins called potins were cast by metallurgists in Britain around 80 BC, probably by the Kentish Canti tribe, the workmanship was rudimentary by comparison with the stater.

Gold Stater, Phillip of Macedonia

The technology for producing the potin would have arrived with the first waves of Belgic invaders, who settled in present-day Sussex, Berkshire, and Hampshire. The coin was an alloy of bronze with a high percentage of tin – there was plenty of alluvial tin to be found in south-west England. At this stage, the notion of stamping a leader's profile on a coin had not started, and typically a god like Apollo would feature on one side with a bull, a boar, or a horse on the reverse.

One of those tribes of invaders, the Atrebates ('settlers'), stood up to Julius Caesar as he fought his way through Gaul, providing a formidable force of 15,000 men. Discretion being the better part of valour, Caesar backed off and waited until the opposing soldiers had drifted back to their farms and settlements before picking them off one by one, finally defeating

Potin

the Atrebates, who had joined forces with the Nervii and the Viromandui among others, at the Battle of Sabis in northern France in 57 BC. Caesar appointed Commios as ruler of the Atrebates and sent him as his envoy to Britain in 55 BC, in advance of his first expedition to try to persuade the Britons not to resist his invasion. However, Commios was promptly captured by the Britons, who hoped to dissuade Caesar from attacking. Of course, that plan failed, Commios was released, and he went on to help Caesar's legions resist further attacks. Commios excelled again during the second Roman expedition to Britain in 54 BC, when he negotiated the surrender of Cassivellaunus, the chieftain who led an alliance of tribes against the Romans. Commios was left in charge and in due course declared himself King of Atrebates, controlling a territory comprising present-day Surrey, West Sussex, and Hampshire.

Com Commios

Coins, now also in gold and silver, stamped with Commios's name and issued from the large Roman town Calleva Atrebatum, have been recovered as well as other coins stamped 'Com Commios,' probably indicating the son of Commios. Later kings, such as Tincomarus, ruler of a kingdom in modern Hampshire and Sussex in the first century BC, Eppillus, and Verica also had their own coins struck with their names, demonstrating some of the earliest writing in Britain.

The author of *Celtic Coinage of Britain*, Robert Van Arsdell, wrote:

> Commios had started the practice by placing his name on the Atrebatic/Regnan staters about 45 BC. Addedormaros promptly responded to this display of vanity by emblazoning his entire name across the Trinovantian/Catuvelliaunian ones. This one-

upmanship game spread quickly to the other tribes and by the end of the millennium all but the Durotrigges and Eceni were striking inscribed types.[1]

Initially, following the Roman invasion, Celtic coins continued to be produced and used, but by the time of Emperor Nero's rule (AD 54–68) they had been phased out. Caesar's preliminary expeditions confirmed that Britain would be a rich source of bounty and trade, but he also records in his *Commentarii de Bello Gallico* how the use of money was still in a primitive stage: 'The number of cattle is great. They use either brass or iron rings, determined at a certain weight, as their money.'[2]

But let us scroll back a little in time to when the Roman legions were still marching through Gaul, pressing north with one eye on Britain; it would be a prestigious prize. When Caesar's legions made their first tentative assault in late summer 55 BC with 10,000 men, establishing a bridgehead of sorts in Kent before retiring across the Channel when bad weather prevented reinforcements arriving, it was enough of an achievement for the Senate in Rome to declare a 20 day holiday.

Faced with a seemingly unstoppable foe, the most natural thing for the hard-pressed Celtic tribes to do when prized possessions were under threat was to hide them. In Jersey, some members of the Coriosolitae, a Gallic tribe from present-day Brittany, decided to bury what they could, planning no doubt to dig it all up later when the threat had passed. Sadly for them the threat never did pass, and one stash of cash – some 50,000 staters and quarter staters worth about £10 million today – remained undiscovered for 2,000 years just three feet beneath a hedge until in 2012 two metal-detecting friends chanced upon the hoard preserved in mud. It was one of the biggest Iron Age finds in Europe, and as one wit put it, possibly the original hedge fund.

The coins were thought to be from a region called Armorica by the Romans, which roughly covers Brittany and Normandy.

1 Robert Van Arsdell, *Celtic Coinage of Britain*
2 Caesar, *Commentarii de Bello Gallico*

Caesar was all too aware that the Britons and Gauls were fighting together against him and the treasure trove found in Jersey itself would seem to confirm that theory. It is also accepted now that there was considerable migration – as opposed to just invasion – from the Continent to Britain. Tacitus, the Roman historian, remarked on the similarity between the Gauls and the people of south-east *Britannia*:

> Their physical characteristics are various and from these conclusions may be drawn. The red hair and large limbs of the inhabitants of Caledonia point clearly to a German origin. The dark complexion of the Silures, their usually curly hair, and the fact that Spain is the opposite shore to them, are an evidence that Iberians of a former date crossed over and occupied these parts. Those who are nearest to the Gauls are also like them, either from the permanent influence of original descent, or, because in countries which run out so far to meet each other, climate has produced similar physical qualities. But a general survey inclines me to believe that the Gauls established themselves in an island so near to them.[3]

Like present day immigrants to Britain, many would simply have arrived and been absorbed into the native population, gradually changing their appearance. It is a process which continues, perhaps even at an accelerated rate, to this day. Nothing lasts forever – especially looks – rather than fight it we should just accept that life has been, is, and will always be, in constant flux.

Another explanation for the numerous hoards of coins found from this period is that they may also have been buried as some sort of religious offering to the gods. On the other hand, perhaps the secret stashes may simply have been abandoned as worthless; as we shall see, coins would fall out of favour and bartering would once again become the normal way of trading for a time. In fact, bartering would survive in parts of Britain well into the 12th century. One of the prime 'currencies' would have been cattle, a word which has the same etymological root as chattel from the

---

3 *Agricola II*

old French and Middle English *chatel* meaning 'property' and the Latin *capitalis*, meaning 'head'. None of the Iron Age tribes that settled in present-day Wales produced their own coins; in fact, they probably rejected their purchasing power altogether, relying on the barter process. The irony is that the Royal Mint, which produces all British coins today, is now in Llantrisant, South Wales. It began transferring its operations there in 1968, finally completing the move to a single site in 1980 employing nearly 1,000 people; it was instantly and wickedly called 'the hole with the mint,' even by the Welsh.

We put a value of £10 million today on the Coriosolitae Jersey find, but what was the real value of money around 100 BC, and how was it valued? To begin with, the first coins represented status and power, and were too valuable to 'waste' on buying goods. Bartering was the norm; far better to trade corn, hunting dogs, or a few captive prisoners snatched on a raiding party from some neighbouring tribe than part with coins. Life was rural and it was also fierce. In 2011, at Fin Cop in Derbyshire, archaeologists uncovered the scene of a massacre. The remains of women, children and babies, stripped of any ornaments, were found dumped in a ditch surrounding a hill fort and crushed under rocks from a stone wall which had been pushed on top of them.

Britain at the time was essentially a land of small farming communities whose lives centred on the seasonal changes, their crops, livestock, and religious festivals. It was a simple existence with basic wooden utensils, leather and bark pots, and tools such as axes and knives fashioned out of iron smelted in primitive clay stoves. The few scraps of clothing that have survived were of wool, skins, and fur, sometimes held in place by a simple brooch or buckle. This was a time when life expectancy was 40 if you were lucky, and malnutrition would have been commonplace; ostentation in clothing or jewellery would have been rare.

Those who could afford the ornate brooches we have since discovered would have been the most powerful chieftains and kings, and those items would have been highly prized. So the moneyers, who actually minted coins, were regarded as magicians, jealously guarding their secrets as they 'struck' the hot molten metal with hammers to 'reveal' the image of gods or animals. But the iron rings, to which Caesar so disparagingly referred, were sometimes quite decorative and ornate objects, such as neck torcs, armbands, and ankle bracelets called La Tène art today, and were crafted with much technical skill considering the rudimentary tools available.

The coins that did exist would more likely have been used to reward the most loyal warriors such as those who helped fight the powerful Diviciacus, King of the Suessiones (Soisson in northern France), or the followers of tribal leaders, from Addedormaros in the North Thames region to Vodenos in the South East. Addedormaros became King of the Trinovantes in 25 BC and almost immediately moved his base from near the River Lea to what is now Colchester. Vodenos was King of the Cantiaci, ruling from about 1 BC to AD 15, and all we know about him is based on the coins he issued, as gradually from c.30 BC initials of rulers, and sometimes the names where the coins were minted, began to be added to the coinage.

A rare find in Dover, Kent, in 2010 suggests the intriguing idea that political coalitions are nothing new. A gold coin stamped with the name of a previously unknown King, Anarevito, as well as EPPI for Eppillus indicates that the two men may have somehow shared power over their territories in Kent and Hampshire between 10 BC and AD 20. One suggestion is that Anarevito may have been the son of Eppillus, but there is no inscription of the letter 'F' for the Latin *filius* (son). The coalition theory of mutual support, in a land where life was short and threats loomed large, remains an appealing notion.

The actual value of the coin during this time was in its weight, and the production was an exact art. In essence, small lumps of precisely weighed gold or silver would be placed in a clay pellet-mould and melted in a furnace. The next stage was to hammer the metal into blanks which would then be struck with dies to create the coin. The varying size and depth of the pellet-moulds would be used for the various weights and denominations of the coins. This was no small scale operation, as it has been suggested that coins in their thousands were being produced by moneyers in different tribes, all doubtless using the same basic techniques. The designs were relatively sophisticated and detailed which undermines the belief that the natives of Britain were mere long-haired, wild people.

Lest we get too carried away with the importance Romans set on Britain we should remember that it was considered a mere province of Rome – *Provincia Britannia* – and probably viewed as nothing more than a source largely of tin; we were a tin mine in other words, with a population of uncouth savages according to Tacitus. But we were also a source of revenue for Rome. Caesar imposed a heavy tax on the tribes before he left in 54 BC, which Cassivellaunus, principal chief of a grouping of Celtic tribes, would have raised from his followers and neighbouring tribes. Nobody would have wanted the Romans back, and it probably seemed like a price worth paying for a period of peace. Numismatists suggest that this annual taxation explains the significant finds of gold staters at Whaddon Chase, Buckinghamshire, South Norfolk, and elsewhere, which can all be dated to a period soon after 54 BC.[4]

Two main tribes rose to prominence in the vacuum left after Caesar's departure, and the coins we now have tell compelling stories about their rivalry fought from the north and south sides of the Thames; to the north was King Tasciovanus, and to the south, King Commios. The coins of both kings and their descendants bore their names and emblems – vine leaves or barley – and occasionally military scenes. But in the end it was the tribes from the north, descendants of King Tasciovanus, who came to dominate and were all powerful by the time the Romans returned.

It would be nearly 100 years after Caesar's first visit before the Emperor Claudius decided in AD 43 to begin his conquest of Britain, led by Aulus Plautius. In classic political diversionary style, it was probably as much to achieve a victory in a foreign adventure to counter the opposition he was getting from the Senate as for any other reason. The Roman Empire was already vast and overstretched; there was little strategic value in crossing the Channel.

4 Chris Rudd, *Journal of Ancient Numismatics*.

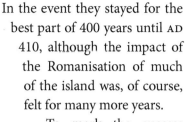

De Brittanis

In the event they stayed for the best part of 400 years until AD 410, although the impact of the Romanisation of much of the island was, of course, felt for many more years.

To mark the success of his invasion, Claudius built an arch in Rome in AD 51 which is featured on the reverse of a gold coin and inscribed DE BRITANNIS, with the Emperor and a victor's laurel wreath on the obverse.

The Romans allowed some tribal leaders to continue to rule so long as they towed the line. One such tribe was the Iceni (also Eceni) in East Anglia, whose chief was Prasutagus. But on Prasutagus's death in AD c.60, Emperor Nero's agents seized the land in accordance with Roman law, and in an ill-judged act of brutality, flogged Prasutagus' widow, Boudicca, and raped her daughters for protesting. The wrath of Boudicca was swiftly unleashed while the Roman Governor, Gaius Suetonius Paullinus, was away fighting the Ordovices in Anglesey. Boudicca, supported by the Trinovantes, swept through Colchester, Verulamium (St Albans), and London in her chariot exacting terrible vengeance. She was eventually defeated at an unknown battlefield in the Midlands by Paullinus on his return from North Wales, but she took her own life rather than risking being captured. Her actions are remembered in the powerful bronze statue bestriding her chariot on Victoria Embankment in London, beside the Houses of Parliament. Perhaps she is challenging those inside to behave with the same fearless courage she displayed in protecting the honour of her own kith and kin.

In 2009, more than 800 gold staters were discovered in a field near Wickham Market, Suffolk. They were probably minted just prior to Queen Boudicca's rule, but it certainly points to the economic and political importance of the region at the time. The hoard, buried in a pottery vase, was probably a votive offering as Snettisham, some 80 miles away, was known to be a major religious centre.

This was a time of great unrest throughout the Roman Empire, and the revolt by the Iceni was matched elsewhere as Nero's increasingly ineffectual and brutal rule fell apart; he was finally driven out of Rome by the Praetorian Guard in AD 68 before committing suicide.

Much of the conquest of Britain was under Gnaeus Julius Agricola, Tacitus's father-in-law. He led his army through Wales, northern England and into Scotland, reaching as far as northern Scotland, attaining victory at the Battle of Mons Graupius AD c.83 as indicated by the discovery of Roman coins in the Scottish Lowlands from this time. But no sooner had he achieved that then he was recalled to Rome.

By AD 105 the Picts, tribes from eastern and northern Scotland, began to push back. Roman forts were destroyed either from attacks or deliberately by the Romans to prevent them falling into the hands of the enemy, and a new line of defence was established further south along the Stanegate, or 'stone road', through the valleys of the Rivers Tyne and Irthing.

Emperor Hadrian decided that a proper defensive position should be built to keep out the 'barbarians from the north,' and by AD 128 his eponymous wall, running 73 miles from Segedunum at Wallsend on the River Tyne to the Solway Firth, was completed.

The practicalities of manning such a construction do not appear to make much sense, and it is now thought that the wall was not so much to keep the enemy out as to collect some form of customs tax, particularly as people passed through its gates going about their everyday business. It wasn't just a stone wall; there were taverns and shops along its way encouraging trade on

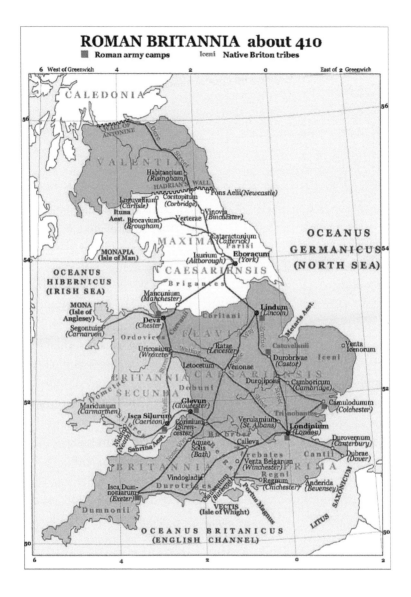

ROMAN BRITANNIA about 410

■ Roman army camps   Iceni Native Briton tribes

6 West of Greenwich   4   2   0   East of 2 Greenwich

CALEDONIA

WALL OF ANTONINE

56

VALENTIA

Habitancium (Risingham)

HADRIAN'S WALL

Pons Aelii (Newcastle)

Luguvallium (Carlisle)   Corstopitum (Corbridge)

Ituna Aest.   Brocavium (Brougham)   Verterae   Vinovia (Binchester)

MAXIMA   Cataractonium (Catterick)

Parisi

OCEANUS GERMANICUS (NORTH SEA)

MONAPIA (Isle of Man)   Isurium (Aldborough)   Eboracum (York)

CAESARIENSIS

OCEANUS HIBERNICUS (IRISH SEA)

Brigantes

Mancunium (Manchester)

MONA (Isle of Anglesey)

Lindum (Lincoln)

Metaris Aest.

Segontium (Carnarvon)

Deva (Chester)

Coritani

Ordovices

FLAVIA

Uriconium (Wroxeter)   Ratae (Leicester)   Catuvellauni   Venta Icenorum

Iceni

Letocetum   Venonae   Durobrivae (Castor)

BRITANNIA CAESARIENSIS

Dobuni   Duroliponte   Camboricum (Cambridge)

Maridunum (Carmarthen)   Glevum (Gloucester)

Isca Silurum (Caerleon)   Corinium (Cirencester)   Trinobantes   Camulodunum (Colchester)

Verulamium (St. Albans)   Londinium (London)

Aquae Solis (Bath)   Calleva   Durovernum (Canterbury)

Sabrina Aest.   Atrebates   Cantii   Dubrae (Dover)

BRITANNIA SECUNDA   Venta Belgarum (Winchester)   Regni

Isca Dumnoniorum (Exeter)   Vindogladia   Durotriges   Anderida (Bevensey)

Regnum (Chichester)   Portus Magnus

Dumnonii   VECTIS (Isle of Wight)

LITUS SAXONICUM

OCEANUS BRITANICUS (ENGLISH CHANNEL)

both sides. The only coins being used in Scotland were Roman; the Scots would have to wait until 1124 before their first coin was minted in the name of their own King, David I, and if they weren't using coins they would have been bartering.

Hadrian was succeeded by his adopted son Antoninus Pius, whose reign was almost entirely peaceful with the curious exception of Britain, where he commanded the Governor, Quinbrus Lollius Urbicus, to push north into Scotland. He had some success, and even built the Antonine Wall near the Forth of Clyde – from present-day Glasgow to Edinburgh – for his Emperor, but once again there were more pressing demands for the legionnaires elsewhere, and the wall was abandoned just 20 years later.

Oddly, despite the mass of Celtic coins recovered, we do not know what the people of *Provincia Britannia* actually called their coins. The Romans had the *denarius*, a small silver coin meaning 'containing 10' as in ten *asses*, which later gave Britain the 'd' for the old penny before decimalisation in 1971, as well as the Arabic *dinar* and the Spanish *dinero*, and the *libra* (pound), which gave the British the old £SD as in pounds, shillings and pence. Collectors today use the terminology of staters, quarter staters, silver units, minims, and potins, but how the Celtic tribes themselves referred to them we do not know. What the coins do tell us is something about the economy of the time. When gold bullion was in short supply after the first Roman invasion, the weight was reduced and ultimately only silver coins were minted. The influence of Roman design on coinage also reflects the extent of the Roman conquests – unsurprisingly, for example, the Iceni designs were most un-Roman in appearance.

Britain was later divided into two provinces, Britannia Superior and Britannia Inferior, (AD c.305), but what is clear from burial sites is that the island was already what would be called today an increasingly multi-cultural society, which is natural for an island nation. It would have been easier to sail across the Channel or the North Sea than to trek across land. Archaeologists studying the Lankhills Roman Cemetery in Winchester have been able to establish that at least quarter of the population was already made up of people who had spent part of their early lives in northern Europe. The Channel was no real obstacle and interaction with the Continent was normal. The gradual withdrawal of Roman forces from Britain began around AD 383 until AD 410, when the last soldiers left, summoned home for various campaigns to protect the Rhine from the Germanic barbarian hordes and Italy from the

Visigoths (but not in time to prevent the Sack of Rome). It left the island wide open to waves of invaders. The gene pool was about to change radically – full scale Europeanisation, as one might say, was now to begin in earnest.

2 ANGLO-SAXON KINGS
AD 410–1066

Britain had been shedding the Roman cloak for years before the final withdrawal in AD 410. The Picts, north of Hadrian's Wall, and the Scots (*Scotti* to the Romans) from Ireland, had been attacking continually until the Great Pict War in AD 367, effectively rendering the border a no-go area for the Romans. In AD 383, General Magnus Maximus, a Spaniard, declared himself Emperor of Britain in defiance of Emperor Gratian, and four years later took much of an already depleted force with him in an ambitious plan eventually to seize Rome itself. He failed, and following his defeat at the Battle of Save by the Eastern Emperor, Theodosius I[5], supported by Hun mercenaries in AD 388, he was captured and executed near Aquileia. It was not long before the Western Emperor, Honorius, called the remaining troops back and told Britain it would have to fend for itself. Thereafter, with the link to the Continent broken, few new Roman coins would reach Britain.

Magnus Maximus

Coins from Maximus's reign have been found, including examples of the *siliqua*, the name given to a silver coin produced from the 4th century onwards. These coins may have been among the first to be used by the Anglo-Saxons, not only as currency but also as also pendants and jewellery. Equally, as the Dark Ages encroached, many of the recovered *siliquae* are seen to have been 'clipped,' suggesting that their owners were more interested in maximising the silver value contained in the coins rather than

---

5 The term emperor is a modern construction. After the first 300 years of the empire and with the increase of rebellious elements along its vast borders in the late 3rd century there was often more than one emperor.

using them to buy goods. Also, with coinage in short supply, and certainly not being replaced as it wore out, what was not buried for a rainy day needed to last. In time coins would once again temporarily slip out of use, or where they were used they would have amounted to tokens, poor replicas of what had once been official coinage. Numismatists can only speculate:

> Just how long money continued to be used is guesswork. It probably went on into the very early years of the sixth century. By then, with nothing to buy, no taxes to pay, no business to conduct and society in disarray, money as such would have had little meaning. Survival itself would have been difficult enough.[6]

So who was running the country now the Roman legions had departed? Essentially it was lawless, with rival tribes competing to win new territory or hold on to what they had seized. Vortigen, King of Kent and 'High Chief' among a group of Celtic tribes in AD 449, felt under increasing pressure from the Picts and asked for help from the Jutes, a Germanic people from the Jutland Peninsula, present-day Denmark and Germany. But, in a parallel with recent history, he should have been wary of the apparent allies he looked to for support. . The Jute mercenaries together with Angle, Saxon and Frisian armies duly fought off the Picts and Scots only to turn on Vortigen and install the brothers Hengist and Horsa as the new rulers in AD c.460. Although some even doubt the existence of the brothers,[7] it is clear that the Jutes were now in charge. Slowly but surely the native Celtic people would be driven westwards further into Wales by the invading forces. Britain was about to become a nation ruled by Germans, but such is the paucity of contemporary literature at the time, hence the Dark Ages, much of the information about daily life has to be conjecture.

For simplicity's sake, we may divide the country away from the even more lawless north into seven kingdoms, all of which were ruled by German kings: Kent, Sussex, Wessex, Essex, Northumberland, East Anglia, and Mercia.

---

6 www.numsoc.net
7 According to popular legend Horsa was buried at Horsenden Hill, Middlesex.

Kent: Following the conquest by Hengist and Horsa, it is thought that Kent was formerly founded by Oisc, son or even grandson of Hengist, in AD c.488, although there were a number of leaders who may have called themselves king of Kent.

Sussex: One assumes word spread among the Saxons that there were rich pickings to be had in Britain following the successful battles of Hengist and Horsa; Ella, a south Saxon, landed at Pevensey Bay (Eastbourne), and after many months of fighting created what became Sussex (south Saxons) in AD 477.

Wessex: In AD 495 more Saxons arrived, landing in the area of Southampton. They marched on and captured Winchester. Cerdic is regarded as the first Saxon King and came to the throne in AD 495. From him it is possible to trace all future kings and queens of England. We have to wait until Alfred the Great (AD 871-899) before we have the first king of all England.

Essex: The last of the Saxons to arrive approached along the Thames Estuary and established the kingdom of Essex in AD 527.

Northumberland: Not wanting to miss out on the opportunity, the Angles sailed across the North Sea, landing north of the Humber in AD 547, establishing Northumbria.

East Anglia: Just 30 years later two more tribes of Angles landed in AD 575 and settled creating what would become Norfolk and Suffolk

Mercia: The last of the seven kingdoms was established in the Midlands by the Angles

By the end of these invasions there were probably some 200,000 Angles, Saxons, and Jutes living in the country – immigration on a grand scale for the time. The result of so many rulers and kingdoms was there was no overall government or 'national' authority, and one of the consequences was that money, where it was in circulation, ceased to be used in the sense of a proper currency. Trade with the Continent dried up, which can be demonstrated by the fact that the coins – *solidi* and *siliquae* – since uncovered date from the period of Magnus Maximus's rule. Vikings – before they invaded Britain – would not have been overly familiar with coins as a currency. They would have been seen as another form of bullion or precious metal, which more often than not would have been melted down to create a piece of jewellery to show off their personal wealth – Viking bling.

Eadbald (AD 616–640), son of the Jute King of Kent, Ethelbert, issued the first coin by an English (albeit only Kent) king; up until then Saxons had been relying on imported Merovingian Frankish[8] coins, which in itself tells us about trade outside Britain. The gold thrymsa, an imitation of Roman bronze coins still in circulation, had a cross on the reverse; this may give us some clue about the development of Christianity in the country. In his early life, Eadbald was a pagan and married his stepmother on his father's death, but later, according to the writings of the Venerable Bede, 'renouncing his unlawful marriage he embraced the faith of Christ and being baptized, promoted the affairs of the church to the utmost of his power.'[9] In fact his father, Ethelbert, was among the first converts to Christianity, baptised by Augustine, who later became the first Archbishop of Canterbury in AD 601.

However, the thrymsa never reached the status of a national, or even regional, currency, and it was not long before it was replaced by the sceatta. This would form the foundation of the whole nation's currency until the 14th century. The gradual reduction in the gold content of the thrymsa to the largely silver sceatta points to the decline in gold bullion arriving from the Continent. The Britons, however, were focussing on fighting their immediate neighbours until one of them became the winner; the dominant forces increasingly were the kings of Northumbria

8 Originally Germanic tribes whose descendants would form the Holy Roman Empire.
9 Venerable Bede, *The Ecclesiastical History of the English People*

who, between AD 613 and AD 731, ruled the whole of England except Kent.

Among them was Ethelfrith, an Angle, who was redoubtable in battle and greatly expanded the territory under his rule to include Bernicia and Deira, which would later become Northumbria.

Another Northumbrian coin to mention in passing is the humble styca, the lowest value coin; worth just half a farthing and made of brass and a zinc, it is probably most notable because so many were produced by multiple moneyers to meet demand during the reigns of Aethelred I, Raedwulf, and Aethelred II.

Sceattae, Aethelred I

But power would shift to Mercia and from it a fascinating and ironic tale about a single coin would emerge, which tells us much about the interests and experiences of the English people.

The first notable King of Mercia is Penda, a man who enjoyed his battles. It is not certain when he became King, but he was

Lunette penny, Aethelred I

victorious in the Battle of Cirencester in AD 628, and defeated his rival, King Edwin of Northumbria, in AD 633 at the Battle of Hatfield. He followed that up with another victory, probably in alliance with Welsh fighters, over Edwin's successor, Oswald, nine years later at the Battle of Maserfield. There was no longer any doubt which king ruled supreme, and he continued fighting his neighbouring Bernicians until he himself was finally defeated and killed by Oswin of Northumbria at the Battle of Winwaed in AD 655. Northumbria would briefly gain the upper hand but it was not long before Penda's son, Wulfhere, restored the Mercian position. Sceattae inscribed with Penda's name underline the dominance of Mercian control at the time.

Although Penda was a pagan, in later life he became tolerant towards Christianity. His son, Peada, converted to Christianity,

which leads us to the curious story of the rare gold coin in the British Museum.

Under Mercian rule Christianity began to flourish; indeed, Aethelred I, another of Penda's sons, abdicated and retired to a monastery, as did one of his grandsons, Coenred, who renounced the throne and left for Rome. But it was in the reign of Offa (AD 757–796), the greatest of the Mercian kings, that the strangest coin emerged and typically has provoked much speculation among numismatists. For modern readers, living in a world of Middle Eastern unrest and ever present threat from terrorism, it is extraordinary.

Offa, famous for Offa's Dyke, the great earthwork constructed along the border between England and Wales, was undoubtedly Christian and eager to be seen as close to the Church in Rome. He wanted Pope Adrian I to appoint an archbishop in Mercia, and did his utmost to win favour with the Vatican. Presumably he asked the papal legates in his court how he could demonstrate his gratitude and they suggested he should send 365 *mancuses* (gold coins), one for every day of the year as alms for the poor – possibly the origins of 'Peter's Pence'.

The issue then was how the gold coins should be inscribed. The result as can be seen on the only remaining coin from the time reads in Arabic letters: 'There is no Deity but Allah, The One, Without Equal, and Muhammad is the Apostle of Allah.' It continues around the margins: 'Muhammad is the Apostle of Allah, Who sent him [Muhammad] with the doctrine and true faith to prevail over every other religion.' Not exactly the most tactful message to send to a pope.

The PR gaffe, as one might generously call it today, may simply have been the result of Offa inquiring what should be sent and the papal legates saying 'make it something like this'. Then someone in the Royal Mint, who could not read Arabic, faithfully followed the writing.

Other explanations include the coins being struck for pilgrims to use in the Holy Land, although it is unlikely that the King would hand out money for such a journey; in any case, the more common coinage struck during Offa's reign were silver 'pennies'. Some have even suggested that Offa had converted to Islam, but this does not make sense given his desire to be close to Rome, the numerous examples of coins from the period showing a cross, and the production of those coins in Canterbury under the auspices of the Archbishop. Most likely it was meant to be a minting specifically for the purpose of sending his tribute to the Pope.

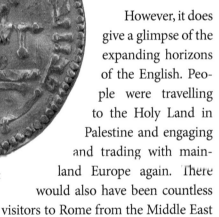

Offa's mancus – an imitation dinar

However, it does give a glimpse of the expanding horizons of the English. People were travelling to the Holy Land in Palestine and engaging and trading with mainland Europe again. There would also have been countless visitors to Rome from the Middle East who would have brought offerings – no doubt including gold coins – for the Pope. One wonders what the Pope would have made of these offerings if anyone had bothered to translate them. When the legates suggested, as we presume, that Offa should send 'something like these' to Rome, they were probably referring to the quality of design and, most importantly, the quality and weight of the gold.

The House of Wessex The Mercian rule came to an end under Egbert (AD 802–839) of Wessex. He had been forced into exile in

France by Offa, in collusion with Beorhtric of Wessex, in the AD 780s, but when Beorhtric died in AD 802, Egbert returned and claimed the throne. He then set about defeating other Mercian leaders including Wiglaf in AD 829, effectively taking control of the whole of South East England. He was declared Bretwalda, or 'Ruler of Britain,'[10] and issued coins proclaiming himself King of Mercia. He pushed home his advantage AD c.830, taking Welsh territory previously under Mercian control. The success of his campaigning was in part due to the support he enjoyed from Louis the Pious, King of the Franks, whom he knew from his time in exile. Indeed his subsequent defeat was no doubt due to the collapse of that support when Louis faced problems of his own at home and called his army back.

The House of Wessex was now firmly in control. King Aethelwulf (AD 839–858), Egbert's son, was a deeply religious man, sending one of his sons, the future King Alfred, to Rome at the age of four. His ring, kept at the British Museum, has religious motifs and a penny coin struck with his name has a cross on the reverse. Although Aethelwulf does not always get a good press, historians agree that he laid the foundations for a long period of Wessex domination which would continue for the next 160 years. He conquered the kingdom of Kent, subjugated Wales, and fought off attacks from the Danes. But the Vikings were beginning to make their presence felt even while he was still alive and his sons, four of whom would succeed him, were kept busy in constant battles.

Coins of the time point to the curious line of succession to Aethelbald (AD 858–860). He tried to usurp his father while he was away on pilgrimage to Rome. On his return Aethelwulf allowed his son to remain as King of Wessex while he retained power in Kent. The only coins to have been discovered all have Aethelwulf's name, which may suggest who still held the upper hand.

When Aethelbald died childless, another of Aethlwulf's sons, Aethelbert (AD 860–865), succeeded him and decided that, unlike his father and brother who separated the 'kingships' of Wessex and Kent, the 'kingdom' should be united.

---

10 *Anglo-Saxon Chronicle* – A history of the Anglo Saxons created in 9th Century.

The 'unification' process continued when his brother, Aethlred I (AD 866–871), succeeded him and introduced a joint currency for Wessex and Mercia with the lunette penny AD c.867.[11] But the Viking threat was growing. They defeated Aethelred's brother-in-law Burgred, the King of Mercia, and in the AD 870s began winning important victories in Wessex, although Aethelred managed to hold the line until his death.

He was succeeded by his brother, Alfred (AD 871–899), who, after some defeats, eventually repelled the Vikings by force of arms and by treaty, declaring himself the first 'King of the Anglo-Saxons,' and of course in time became known as Alfred the Great. Alfred's exceptional achievements in legal reform, military organisation, and education are fully documented, as well as the long period of peace he delivered against the Viking threats. One interesting and misleading coin in the Royal Mint from his reign points to his consolidation of power beyond Wessex and into

Silver penny, Alfred the Great

London. A silver penny monogrammed *Londonia* suggests that this was struck to mark the 'restoration' of London under his authority in AD 886. But London was already under Alfred's influence through his ally, Ceolwulf II, King of Mercia (AD 874–879), and together they issued coinage during this time. The silver penny in question is more likely to be linked to more mundane repair work carried out by Alfred after a Viking raid.[12]

Ceolwulf II, Watlington Hoard

In 2015 a hoard of Viking coins was dug up in a field in Oxfordshire; both Alfred and Ceolwulf were depicted on the

11 Geoffrey Hindley, *A Brief History of the Anglo-Saxons* (London: Robinson, 2006).
12 D. Keynes, *Kings, Currency and Alliances* (Woodbridge: Boydell Press, 1998).

same coins, which scholars suggest proves that Ceolwulf was a much more prominent king than previously believed. 'Here is a more complex political picture in the 870s which was deliberately misrepresented in the 890s after Alfred had taken over the whole of Ceolwulf's kingdom,' said Dr. Gareth Williams, curator of medieval coinage at the British Museum.[13]

Whatever Alfred did not control one way or another was under the rule of the Vikings, known as Danelaw, and this was something his son, Edward the Elder (AD 899–924), set about changing with the help of his sister, Ethelflaed. She was married to Ethelred, who ruled Mercia by royal appointment as an 'Ealdorman'. On Ethelred's death Ethelflaed in effect became the ruler, dubbed 'Lady of the Mercians,' and fought with Edward against the Danes. The coins issued in Mercia at the time, most probably under Ethelflaed's instructions, bear her brother's name.

By AD 918 Edward had resisted a challenge to his position from his cousin, Ethelwold, who was supported by the Danes. He had defeated the Danes south of the Humber and was eventually acknowledged as 'father and lord' by the Norse, Welsh, and Scots. For the first time Scotland was under the authority of an English king; just over a thousand years later nearly half of Scots would still be claiming it back in a referendum which narrowly backed retaining the Union.

And so it was that Edward's son, Athelstan (AD 924–939), could rightly claim to be the first King of England once he had defeated the Danes in their last remaining stronghold of York in AD 927, and won the submission of Constantine II, King of Scotland, along with all the Welsh kings. However, he had to wait until AD 925 to be crowned, as his half-brother, Elfweard of Wessex, also claimed the throne only to die within weeks of his father's death.

With such a large kingdom to control, Athelstan, brought in new laws, not least measures to combat fraud regulating the weight of silver coins. The Statute of Greatley, AD 928 decreed that there should be a 'national' currency for England, although coins would remain regionalised for some years to come. Athelstan also had the foresight to realise that Britain would always be a trading nation and established links with Europe by arranging the marriage of four of his half-sisters to rulers in western Europe.

However, the Danes were not done yet, and on Athelstan's death in AD 939, they succeeded in reclaiming York. The new King, Edmund I (AD 939–946), had other enemies closer to home and was murdered in his own hall in Pucklechurch (Gloucestershire), just seven years into his reign. It would be another 15 years before York was retaken. Edmund was succeeded by his son, Edred (AD 946–955).

According to the *Anglo-Saxon Chronicle*, Edred 'reduced all the land of Northumbria to his control and the Scots granted him oaths that they would do all that he wanted'. Even though Edred was a sick man, suffering from an eating disorder, he was no pushover when it came to a fight.

Although he had received due homage from various leaders and kings from Wales and northern England, including the minor kings of Northumbria, there was still rebellion in the air. When the Viking leader, rejoicing in the name Eric Bloodaxe, was invited to become King of Northumbria, supported by Archbishop Wulfstan of York, who had only just pledged his allegiance to the rightful King, Edred exacted terrible vengeance by marching his army north to destroy Ripon and wreak havoc throughout Northumbria. But he was taken momentarily by surprise when his rearguard was attacked. Edred's blood was evidently up because he turned round and pillaged what was left of Northumbria again. Eric Bloodaxe escaped, later managed to return to York as King once more, only to be killed in an ambush along with five other kings. Edred's position was absolute and he issued coins in his name in Northumbria to drive the point home.

Despite his ferocious demeanour on the battlefield, Edred was a supporter of the church and in his final years took much advice from (St) Dunstan, Abbot of Glastonbury, later to become Archbishop of Canterbury.

Still in his thirties, the last warrior-king of Wessex died childless and was succeeded by his 15-year-old nephew, Edwy

(AD 955–959), who is regarded by all as a nasty piece of work. He particularly disliked Dunstan, who had humiliated him by forcing him to spend more time in the council chamber and less time in the bed chamber with Elgifu, who would only later become his wife. But the marriage just made matters worse as she was the daughter of Edwy's former mistress and stepmother, Ethelgiva. Edwy was forced to give up his wife and banish her from court as the church considered the marriage illegitimate because Ethelgiva was the King's third cousin and therefore too close a blood relative. Dunstan realised the wisest course of action was to retreat to a monastery in Ghent while Edwy remained King.

For the rest of his short reign Edwy managed to upset everyone, putting up taxes (a coin was struck in his name), and showing favouritism towards Wessex in preference to the rest of his kingdom. The Mercians and Northumbrians rose in rebellion and eventually forced Edwy to accept his brother, Edgar, as king of all the territory north of the Thames. The circumstances surrounding his death are uncertain; he may have been murdered but he was not mourned.

Edgar 'the Peaceful' (AD 959–975) is remembered for an orderly and indeed peaceful reign, free from outside attack or internal strife. One of his first decisions was to order the recall of Dunstan from his exile and install him first as Bishop of Worcester; he then became Bishop of London before finally being enthroned as Archbishop of Canterbury. Not only was this to be an orderly reign – he introduced the concept of shires to England, sub-divided into hundreds – it was to be one founded on strong religious beliefs, not to mention a formidable navy. As for the Vikings, Edgar followed a policy of non-interference in the north and east called Danelaw – you leave us alone and we will leave you alone. It was a policy which worked admirably.

For this story Edgar is notable for introducing what is regarded as the first truly national coinage or currency. Until then coins were regionalised in the sense that they tended to remain largely in the areas where they were produced.

It is thought that Edgar's currency reforms came in AD c.973, in other words towards the end of his reign, lasting until

Henry II ascended the throne. Some forty mints were established throughout the country, producing the same penny coins from centrally distributed dies with Edgar's portrait on the obverse and a small cross on the reverse surrounded by names of the moneyers and mints. While it was an orderly distribution of coinage, fiscal control remained centralised, *plus ça change*.

Unfortunately, Edgar's support of the monasteries, including the distribution of land taken from some of the noble families, would prove to be the undoing of his appointed successor, Edward 'the Martyr' (AD 975–978). Unsurprisingly, the nobles resented what had happened to them and declared that Edward was illegitimate, despite the backing of Archbishop Dunstan, throwing their support behind Edward's younger half-brother, Ethelred (AD 978–1016). They seized back their land and, in mysterious circumstances, Edward was murdered at Corfe Castle in Dorset.

However, at just 10 years or possibly a little older, Ethelred II was indeed 'the Unready', although this is regarded as a mistranslation of the Old English *unraed* meaning 'ill-advised'. Either way, the Danes spotted a weakness, launched a series of prolonged attacks which only paused for a time when Ethelred agreed to pay a bounty – Danegeld. As usual the proof lies in the vast quantities of Anglo-Saxon pennies found in Denmark. It is estimated that during his reign, Ethelred paid 40 million pennies to bribe the Vikings not to attack – roughly the equivalent of £150,000 of silver.

The peace did not last, and provoked by the massacre of Danes on St Brice's Day in 1002, a large Danish army returned and drove Ethelred out of the country in 1013, leaving England nominally ruled by King Sweyn of Denmark. But he died soon afterwards and Ethelred was able to return from Normandy.

The coinage minted during Ethelred's reign still reflects some Roman influence, with images of him in a tunic and based on 4th century Roman coins. In addition, a large gold cross appears on some coins, which facilitated breaking the coins into quarters as much as reflecting any religious significance. Clearly the weight of the coinage was still just as important as its nominal value.

Ethelred's reign fell apart when Sweyn died and one of his sons, Canute (Cnut) the Great, began what would turn out to be a long series of battles supported at times by English nobles. But Canute was not ready for a full-scale battle, and when he withdrew temporarily, Ethelred made the kingdom of Lindsey, which lay between the Wash and the Humber, pay the price for siding with the Danish leader.

Canute returned in 1015 with a formidable force of 10–20,000 Vikings aboard their longships, supported by Polish allies. In a series of battles – mostly against Ethelred's son, Edmund Ironside – over the next 14 months, Canute eventually conquered much of England, as one by one the West Saxons, Northumbrians, and Mercians submitted to him. In 1016 Ethelred died, and in a temporary pact, the country was divided between Canute and Edmund. But it was a short lived arrangement and the briefest of reigns for Edmund because Canute defeated him at the Battle of Ashingdon on 18 October 1016. Edmund died just over a month later, bringing an end to the long, unbroken rule of the House of Wessex.

The House of Denmark Canute (1016–1035) was now King of England, striking a coin as 'King of the English' to mark the occasion, and set about building alliances to protect himself. Malcolm of Scotland paid him due homage; he immediately married Emma of Normandy, Ethelred's widow, and then married a second wife, Elfgifu of Northampton, mother of the future Harold I. The arrangement did not sit well with the church but Canute would keep his two 'wives' apart and bestow generous gifts on the church during his reign, eventually bringing Christianity to Scandinavia.

On the death of his brother, Harald II, in 1018 he became King of Denmark. Within 10 years he was also King of Norway

Penny, Canute

and parts of Sweden, which he achieved through diplomacy and treaties rather than force, and yet we still only remember him for his apparent folly in trying to order back the waves.

In reality the story, according to the 12th century historian Henry of Huntingdon, was an attempt by Canute to demonstrate to his overly fawning courtiers that a king's power was as nothing compared to God's – not even a king could command the tides. 'Let all men know how empty and worthless is the power of kings,' he is said to have declared.[14] He ruled for 19 years and during that time brought peace to the country once again, free from the threat of Viking Invasion.

Despite his ruthlessness in dispatching English nobles he perceived to be rivals, he succeeded in bringing stability to his extended kingdom, uniting Britain and much of Scandinavia, as well as introducing and strengthening laws including those relating to the currency.

Confident of his position, he raised a mighty sum in Danegeld, the equivalent of £72,000, paid off most of his army, and sent them home, retaining only a few ships to discourage any outside threat.

The problem with a large empire is that lines of communication and authority can become stretched. While being distracted by England, there was a move by some to install Canute's son, Harthacanut, who was still a child, as King of Denmark. Canute saw off the threat by sailing straight back to Denmark. Peace once again restored to the kingdom, the deeply religious Canute found time to make his way to Rome to witness the accession of the Holy Roman Emperor, Conrad II, in 1027. On his way back he wrote an 'open' letter to his people signed: 'king of all England and Denmark and the Norwegians and some of the Swedes.' His authority was complete.

On Canute's death in 1035 there followed a thirty-year period of unrest with multiple quests for the throne of England; at each turn it was marked by the minting of new coins. Between Edgar's reign and the 1150s there were around 50 changes, including 14

14 *Chronicle of the History of England*

between Canute's death and 1066. These changes kept the mints busy, reflecting the uncertainty and instability in the country.

Denmark was continuously under threat from Norway and Sweden; this threat was increasing at the time of Canute's death. One of his son's, Harthacnut, who had already been declared King of Denmark by his father, found himself too distracted by the attacks to pay much attention to England; his half-brother, Svein, had lost control of Norway and had fled to Harthacnut's court. In Harthacnut's absence support shifted in England to Svein's full brother, Harold Harefoot who was first appointed Regent and then King in 1037.

However, it was a short reign, and Harthacnut waited until Harold died in 1040 to assume the English throne. Whether it had always been intended that Harthacnut should have been King of England as soon after Canute died is uncertain, but in his *Dictionary of National Biography*, M. K. Lawson notes that mints south of the Thames produced silver pennies in Harthacnut's name, while those in the north struck coins in Harold's name.[15] But for two short years England and Denmark had one King again.

Apart from making himself deeply unpopular by increasing taxes to enlarge his fleet, Harthacnut was not a healthy man, and possibly fearing he did not have long to live and to ensure a smooth succession, called his half-brother, Edward, back from Normandy. In June the following year, 1042, Harthacnut died, some say from a stroke after a bout of heavy drinking at a wedding, others that he was suffering from tuberculosis.

Edward the Confessor (1042–1066) assumed the throne and for a time restored the rule of the House of Wessex, albeit relying on the support of the earls of Wessex, Mercia and Northumbria.

However, Edward, the son of Ethelred the Unready, and Emma, daughter of Richard I of Normandy and second wife of Canute, allowed his French connection to influence him. He favoured his Norman friends over the English nobility, including his father-in-law, Godwin, Earl of Wessex. The crisis came to a head when, in 1051, Edward rejected one of Godwin's relatives as Archbishop

---

15 M. K. Lawson, *Dictionary of National Biography*

of Canterbury, choosing instead his own man, Robert, the Abbot of Jumièges. The new Archbishop accused Godwin of plotting against the King and he was forced into exile with his family.

But Godwin was back the following year at the head of an army, and when the earls of Mercia and Northumbria refused to back the King, Edward had no choice but to submit to their demands, including replacing Robert of Jumièges. Godwin died two years later to be succeeded by his son, Harold, but the issue which still remains unclear is who Edward, without a natural heir, wanted to succeed him.

As he retreated more from public life, relying increasingly on the Godwin family to run the affairs of state, some assume that he wanted Harold Godwin, Earl of Essex, to become King on his death, but another theory is that William of Normandy, who may have visited England during Godwin's brief exile, had been promised the throne by Edward at the time. Some accounts even suggest that Harold was sent to Normandy to confirm such a promise.

Although Edward's reign was characterised by difficulties with some of his nobles, it was largely peaceful, and trading with the Continent continued. The coinage was typical, with pennies still being broken up to create halves and farthings rather than producing smaller coins. The recycling of coinage was reduced to less than three years, ensuring more profits rolled into the King's treasury.

Quite whether Edward was a saint, or whether the considerable backing later of Henry II for his canonisation had an influence, one will never know. No matter, on Edward's death in January 1066, the Witan, a council of senior nobles, proclaimed Harold, the last of the House of Wessex, as King; but he must have known that the Normans were coming.

3 NORMANS AND THE ANARCHY
1066–1154

The Normans, we can sometimes forget, were originally Vikings. In AD 911, Rollo had secured a tract of northern France as part of a peace treaty from Charles II of France and the Nor(th) men, or Norsemen, settled in the area. Rollo became the first Duke of Normandy. Over time the Vikings became totally subsumed into the local culture and adopted the French language; it would be a while before the English court actually started speaking English.

In 1066, William, then Duke of Normandy, decided to claim what he thought was rightfully his, the English crown, even if he may have tricked Harold into making such a promise when he had visited.

William chose his moment to attack well. Harold's own brother, Tostig, had thrown his lot in with Harold Hardrada, King of Norway, who had landed with an invasion force in Yorkshire.

King Harold had no choice but to make the long march north and fight the invaders, which he did, winning a decisive battle at Stamford Bridge, killing both Tostig and Harold Hardrada. Then, of course, he received news that William and his army had landed in Pevensey Bay on 28 September, so Harold had to march his exhausted men all the way back down to Kent. There was only ever going to be one outcome when they met in Hastings; all depicted in the Bayeux Tapestry (actually an embroidery by nuns in Canterbury or Winchester, England, but now hanging in Bayeux Cathedral in France).

With ruthless efficiency, William set about stamping his mark on his new kingdom, building stone castles – including the White Tower of the Tower of London – and cathedrals throughout the land; imposing and strong after the usual Anglo-Saxon wooden structures, they would have left the population in no doubt about the new order. Where there was dissent, and there was for the first

Penny, William I

few years of his reign, it was dealt with mercilessly – such as in the Harrying of the North[16] – and soon insurrection from home and abroad died away.

Over the years he established 70 mints throughout the land to meet high demand – a process that continued during his successor's reign – and issued coins (pennies) in his name, sometimes with his image facing straight on in an uncompromising style and in contrast to the usual profile pose. For many, coins may have been the only image they ever saw of their new King and the message they gave had to be clear. As usual, if smaller units of money were needed the coins would be broken into halves and quarters.

The weight of the coin continued to give it its real value and William was no less ruthless with the many moneyers he employed in production of the coinage. If they produced coins which were underweight punishments were severe, even execution – this probably did not happen very often as the moneyers stamped their names on each coin, so it would be hard to deny the charge. Fraud, like rebellion, soon became a rare event during his reign. Every 2–4 years coins would be recalled and a new minting would take place, allowing the King to take his percentage in the process. It was all part of the control and order William insisted on, not least in his Domesday Book, in

16 When Edwin of Mercia and Morcar of Northumbria rose up in rebellion supported by Danish forces and took the city of York in 1069, William retaliated not only by retaking and destroying York but by destroying anything else in his path in the north of England, something he is said to have regretted later in his dying days.

which he recorded every property in the land from which he drew his taxes.

Governance and administration of his two domains – Normandy and England – were kept separate with separate coinages; English pennies had a higher silver content than the Norman coins and the two never mixed, although on the Continent other currencies were considered legal tender.[17] No-one can be certain, but the origin of the term 'sterling' we still use today may derive from the Latin *librae sterilensium*, referring to the Norman silver penny.[18] Another suggestion by the British numismatist Professor Philip Grierson is that the name derives from the Middle English *ster* meaning 'strong' or 'stout' to reflect that William had sought to improve the quality of the coinage.

William shuttled back and forth between England and France in the early part of his reign, but once he had firmly established control over England by 1072, he spent most of his time on the Continent, in large part dealing with his eldest son, Robert, and his rivalry with his brother, William.

Depending on one's point of view, William I's reign was either a disaster for the English people, imposing a Norman yolk on 'native' Anglo-Saxons, or an innovative force for good which set England fair for the years ahead.

On his death while campaigning in northern France in 1087, William I's estates in Normandy passed to Robert, and William Rufus II (1087–1100) inherited the English crown. Unfortunately, that presented the nobles with lands in both countries with a problem: where should their loyalties lie? Some decided that the two territories had to be reunited again under one ruler and threw their support behind Robert. But Robert's forces were defeated in England when he failed to appear alongside them. William subsequently invaded Normandy and seized territory to shore up his position, although he and his brother were later reconciled.

When Robert decided to depart on the First Crusade, called by Pope Urban II in 1096, he asked William to help him finance the expedition (which William did by raising a punitive tax on the

---

17 David Bates, *William The Conqueror* (Stroud: The History Press, 2008).
18 Term used by the English chronicler Orderic Vitalis (1075–1142).

English) and while he was away, to look after his lands. William now had what he wanted: total control. Robert did not return until after William's death.

But William goes down in history as a ruthless and unpopular King. His 50 mints throughout the land kept producing the coins, and just as swiftly William seemed to gather the money back. The church was not immune from his taxation and he was not averse to delaying making clerical appointments to enable him to divert funds to his coffers, making him especially unpopular with the clergy. When Anselm, the man he had appointed as Archbishop of Canterbury, failed to agree with the king, Anselm decided it would be prudent to seek sanctuary in France, leaving William to enjoy the revenues from the archdiocese.

Nevertheless, for all his faults, William II did manage to extend his power. He repulsed an attack from Malcolm III of Scotland, ventured into Wales (where he built defensive castles), and captured new territory in France.

Anselm's biographer, Eadmer, wrote: '...in war and in the acquisition of territory he enjoyed such success that you would think the whole world smiling upon him.'[19] It wasn't, and in mysterious circumstances William met his end, struck down by an arrow while out hunting. Murder or accident: did one Walter Tirel, an expert bowman, loose the fatal shot? We will never know.

What we do know is that William died without any heirs, prompting his brother, Henry, who was hunting with him, to ride straight for Winchester to seize control of the Treasury. He who controls the purse strings it seems controls the country, and within days he had himself proclaimed King Henry I (1100–1135).

Henry was the poor relation who had missed out when his father, William the Conqueror, divided his lands between his brothers, Robert and William II. He must have felt he was due some reward. Robert, however, had other ideas, and thinking he should have been the rightful King of England on his return from the Crusades, attempted to overthrow his brother in 1101. A temporary truce between them was reached but Robert continued

19 *Life of Anselm*

Penny, Henry I

to push his claims prompting Henry to take his army to Normandy where he defeated Robert at the Battle of Tinchbrai in 1106. Henry kept him prisoner for the rest of his life.

Perhaps the greatest benefit to emerge from Henry's long-running problems in France, perpetuated by the claims of Robert's son, William Clito, to Normandy, supported by Louis VI of France, was that he had to put in place an effective machinery to 'manage' England during his absence, and as ever, money mattered most. He established what we have all come to loathe: an Exchequer supported by a bureaucracy to run the affairs of state. It was responsible for collecting taxes, often rigorously, as well as managing justice. Ingeniously, he did not look to 'the great and the good' among the nobility to fill key posts but appointed largely unknown but able 'new men' to be his administrators – perhaps the first civil servants.

Although the administration was highly efficient the quality of the coins being produced was gradually deteriorating – fraud from underweight coinage was still a problem as it had been during William I's reign. In 1124, 150 moneyers accused of producing underweight coins were hauled before Henry in Winchester – 94 were convicted, had their right hands chopped off, and were castrated.[20] Few coins from Henry's rule have survived – the poor quality pointing perhaps to an impending decline in authority.

---

20 Alan Palmer and Veronica Palmer, *The Chronology of British History* (London: Century Ltd, 1995).

Henry is also credited with introducing the 'tally stick' – an early forerunner of our own credit card system. Coins were not readily available, and most

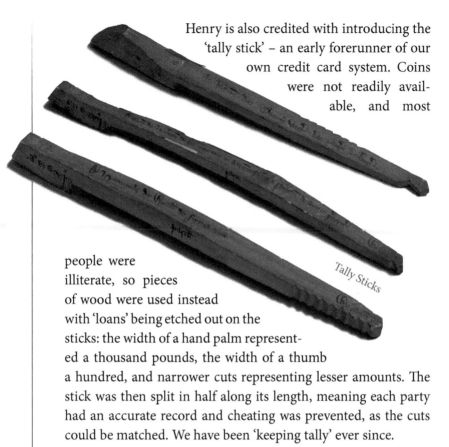

Tally Sticks

people were illiterate, so pieces of wood were used instead with 'loans' being etched out on the sticks: the width of a hand palm represented a thousand pounds, the width of a thumb a hundred, and narrower cuts representing lesser amounts. The stick was then split in half along its length, meaning each party had an accurate record and cheating was prevented, as the cuts could be matched. We have been 'keeping tally' ever since.

Henry had married Matilda, daughter of Malcolm III of Scotland, in all probability a political marriage to consolidate friendship and alliance with a potentially difficult neighbour. But Henry's only legitimate son – he had countless illegitimate sons and daughters by a variety of mistresses – William Adelin drowned when the *White Ship* went down in 1120. Henry married a second time in the hope of producing a son and heir, but Adeliza, daughter of Godfrey I, Count of Louvain, remained childless.

In despair, Henry announced that his daughter, Matilda, should succeed him. But this would prove to be too much for the noblemen of England, who were clearly not ready to be ruled by a queen, and on Henry's death in December 1135, announced that his nephew, Stephen (1135–1154), should be King. The country was about to descend into twenty years of lawlessness dubbed 'the Anarchy,' while according to the 12th century *Peterborough Chronicle*, 'Christ and his saints slept'.[21]

One of Henry's 'new men' in court was David, the youngest son of Malcolm III of Scotland. Until this point no king of Scotland had ever produced his own coinage, but this was about to change with the so-called 'Davidian Revolution'.

From the age of about 16, David had become dependent on the hospitality of Henry's court, having been forced into exile by Donald III of Scotland; in due time he became Prince of the Cumbrians and Earl of Northampton and Huntingdon. When his brother, Alexander I of Scotland, died he sought to succeed him, and with Henry's backing was crowned King in 1124. Drawing on the proceeds of his silver mines in Cumbria, he produced Scotland's first coins – a symbolic and powerful demonstration of his authority.

The Davidian Revolution historians speak about is to do with the radical changes in Scottish government and administration learned from David's time in the court of King Henry, backed by the arrival of French knights. Although he struggled long and hard to subdue his Scottish kingdom, he was not helped by the fact that he was something of an 'absentee landlord', spending much of his time in Henry's court.

But no sooner had David begun to consolidate his position then his backer Henry died. David lent his support to Matilda, Henry's chosen heir, and to that end fought and won new territory against King Stephen's forces in the north of England. Whether his support for Matilda was genuine or whether it was a land grabbing exercise is debatable; suffice it to say that when his and Stephen's armies met on the field at Durham, rather than fight, Stephen agreed to allow David to keep what he had taken in Carlisle and other northern territory.

The truce did not last; emboldened by his success, David launched a series of further attacks deeper into English territory. Battles were fought and often ended with the agreement that David should keep even more land under his authority, which encompassed Northumberland and the country north-west of the Pennines and north-east to the River Tyne.

---

21 *Peterborough Chronicle*

By the time David died in 1153, he was already regarded as a reforming leader, a 'king not barbarous of a barbarous nation,' said William of Newburgh, the 12th century English chronicler.[22]

Stephen was in modern colloquial parlance 'a chancer'. Like David he had been one of the 'new men', brought over from France to Henry's court, and he had sworn allegiance to his cousin, Empress Matilda,[23] as the future Queen of England. He too should have been on the *White Ship* but had chosen to not to travel for unknown reasons. With strong backers, including his brother, Henry of Blois, reputed to be the second richest man in England as well as being Bishop of Winchester and Abbot of Glastonbury, he raced over from France as soon as he heard that Henry I had died and claimed the throne.

As usual the priority was to follow the money, and Stephen made straight for Winchester where Roger, the Bishop of Salisbury as well as Lord Chancellor, ordered that the Treasury should be handed over to Stephen. Helpfully his brother, Henry, ruled that he should never have been made to take the oath swearing allegiance to Matilda and that the nation needed a king because of the unrest. The way was clear to Stephen being crowned King a week later on 22 December at Westminster Abbey.

Stephen's reign was dominated by one long series of battles almost from the moment of his accession, and as leaders throughout history to the present day have found and at times forgotten, warfare is a costly business. If you haven't got the funds you cannot fight the fight. Even the seemingly bottomless pit of his brother's vast fortune would eventually be depleted.

He had his troubles in Scotland with the acquisitive David I, rebellions in Wales, and Robert, Earl of Gloucester and the eldest of Henry's many illegitimate children, declared his support for Matilda in the south-west.

And that was just what was occupying him at home; in France he had a new problem. His cousin, the wilful Matilda, had been forced to marry the teenager, Geoffrey, Count of Anjou, whose lands

---

22 Alan O. Anderson, *Scottish Annals from English Chroniclers* (London: D. Nutt).
23 Matilda claimed the title of Holy Roman Empress through her first marriage to Emperor Henry V.

bordered the Duchy of Normandy, creating a formidable territorial alliance. In due time they had three sons – the future Plantagenet dynasty. No doubt seeking some form of revenge for his wife's loss of the English crown, Geoffrey began a series of raids into Normandy in 1135, destroying what land he could not hold. In 1138, seeing Stephen was occupied by the Earl of Gloucester, he stepped up his attacks. Eventually an agreement was reached to end hostilities, but it cost Stephen the loss of some territory as well as the payment of 2,000 marks a year to Geoffrey in order to keep the peace.

If nothing else Stephen was a fighter and skilled military man, but there are only so many battles one can fight at once. In 1139 Matilda finally arrived in England to claim her crown. At one point she was trapped in Arundel Castle in Sussex, but for reasons that are unclear Stephen agreed to allow her to leave with a few knights and join Robert of Gloucester. Stephen may have thought he wanted to concentrate his forces against Robert rather than divide them up trying to besiege an impregnable castle.

However, Stephen was losing friends. Senior bishops who had been dispossessed of their own castles, private armies, and lucrative domains began to side with Matilda, and nobles, such as Ranulf of Chester, who had seen some of his land handed over to David and his son, Prince Henry, to appease the Scots, spotted an opportunity to regain that land through the Empress.

By 1141, the game was up and at the Battle of Lincoln, Stephen, fighting in the midst of his own men, was surrounded by the superior forces of Robert and Ranulf and taken prisoner.

If there was any doubt about the disarray in the country, one need look no further than the fact that barons and even bishops were now minting their own coins; Prince Henry had rubbed salt in the English wounds by issuing his own coinage. Once again the chaos in the realm is reflected in the different coinages being produced by Matilda and her supporters in the areas they controlled. But Stephen himself was lax:

The traditional practice was that the moneyers were licensed by the crown and supervised by the sheriffs. Stephen, however, is known to have granted to two bishops and one abbot the right to appoint their own moneyers, and it may reasonably be suspected that some of the moneyers in the county boroughs passed, whether by grant or not, under the control of the earls, together with the profits if exchanging old money for new.[24]

However, not everyone was happy to see Matilda crowned, and she was forced to turn back from London as she tried to make her way there for her own coronation. Meanwhile, Stephen's wife, Queen Matilda, kept his flame alive and managed to gather support and forces around her.

When Stephen's brother, Henry, who had been playing both sides, eventually threw his lot in with Queen Matilda, the game changed. At the Rout of Winchester in 1141, Robert himself was captured as he tried to besiege Henry in the city. In a curious deal, it was agreed that Robert and Stephen could be handed back in a sort of exchange of hostages. Stephen was restored to the throne and even held a second coronation ceremony with his Queen Matilda at Christmas.

By 1147 everyone seems to have become war-weary. Nobles were striking deals with the King and each other to hang on to the land they had won, Robert of Gloucester seemed content with his lot and would eventually die peacefully, and Empress Matilda in time returned to Normandy. As we have noted, national currency was in much disarray with nobles still minting their own coins everywhere beyond the immediate south-east.

Stephen's coffers and his regular revenues were severely depleted, and apart from the sporadic incursions from Normandy led by Empress Matilda's son, Henry, no-one was spoiling for a fight. In time all that mattered to Stephen was securing Eustace, his eldest son, as his successor. But when Eustace died early, the question of succession was once again thrown wide open. Although Stephen had a younger son, William, agreement was eventually reached at the Treaty of Winchester in 1153 that Henry, Empress Matilda's son, would be recognised as the rightful heir, bringing an end to years of civil war.

As though to say 'I'm not done yet,' Stephen minted new coins, issued a series of royal writs and travelled round the country to

---

24 Wilfred Lewis Warren, *The Governance of Norman and Angevin England, 1086–1272* (Stanford University Press, 1987).

re-establish order. But he died in the summer of 1154, ushering in the House of Angevin and the Plantagenets.

As we have seen, interaction between the Crown and the church was all important. Kings often appointed clerics to high offices of state just to keep potential rival families and future claimants to the throne at arm's length. After the fall of the Roman Empire it was the church which filled the vacuum as rival kingdoms tried to assert their authority in the land. There was only one recognised religion at the time, Christianity, and everything else was regarded as heresy. The power of the church during this time was all encompassing – if anyone was out of favour with the church they lived in fear of damnation in hell. There was no escape: peasants had to pay taxes (tithes) to the church which was usually in kind because they had little or no actual money. People had to pay to be baptised, to marry, and even to be buried in consecrated ground, and failure to do so led to eternal damnation; almsgiving to pay for a safe passage into heaven was the norm. The boundaries between church and laity were blurred and so long as one wasn't a peasant at the bottom of the pecking order, everyone could exact some form of payment from the lower orders.

This powerful hold over people no matter what their status enabled the church to become extraordinarily wealthy and gave the clergy enormous influence. Property owned by senior members of the church was not exempt though, as even men from these properties had to fight in war. This, of course, was costly and led to more taxation which the church was able to impose. It would still be some years before the archbishops of Canterbury stopped running mints albeit on behalf of the Crown; an archbishop could just as easily be Chancellor of the Exchequer or Lord Chancellor, and controlling the Treasury was vital, as Henry I and Stephen demonstrated.

Senior clergy were invariably drawn from the nobility, and simony was rife. Bishops and archbishops fell in and out of favour with their kings as allegiances and support shifted, sometimes becoming deeply embroiled in political manoeuvring, such as Robert of Jumièges conniving against Godwin, Earl of Wessex, or Henry of Blois 'fixing' it for his brother, Stephen, to become

King and funding his campaigns. At times, when the political tide turned against them, bishops felt the wisest move was to go into exile, leaving behind not only their flocks but also their vast properties, which monarchs duly plundered.

As the largest landowner in Europe the Roman Catholic Church wielded great power over kings and held the ultimate threat of excommunication. As we shall see when King John disagreed with Pope Innocent III over the appointment of an archbishop he was excommunicated, and the time would soon come when church and state would have to be clearly separated. However, there was unease in some quarters of the church that the clergy, from senior bishops to the monks in the monasteries, were more secular than spiritual in their lifestyles, and from the late 10th century new orders sprang up – the Benedictine Reform in England – reintroducing a more austere, contemplative, and spiritual existence.

Kings and emperors across Europe were still reluctant to give up the right to appoint bishops; one of the sticking points along the way was the vast wealth of church properties. But the first sign of a compromise was reached with the Concordat of Worms between Pope Calixtus II and the Holy Roman Emperor Henry V in 1122, which paved the way to the church appointing its own representatives. However, another turbulent priest in England would first have to be dealt with by a disgruntled monarch.

4 THE ANGEVIN EMPIRE AND THE PLANTAGENETS
1154–1399

Not everyone agrees that the Angevin Empire was a true empire, not least because it did not have an emperor, but it was a collection of seven sovereign countries and they did have one head – Henry II (1154–1189), the first Plantagenet King of England, Count of Anjou and Duke of Normandy. Plantagenet derives from the Latin *planta genista,* the yellow broom which according to one theory Geoffrey wore in his hat. Angevin, a term coined in 1887 by Kate Norgate in her book, *England Under the Angevin Kings,*[25] derives from Henry's lands in Anjou. If it wasn't an empire it was certainly a vast territory, stretching from the Pyrenees to Ireland, covering the whole of England and half of France. Four royal houses would now dominate the country for more than 300 years: the Angevins, Plantagenets, Lancastrians, and Yorkists.

Throughout history confidence in the national currency, and by extension, the country itself, has been regarded as paramount; fraud and debased coinages undermined people's willingness to take coins at their face value. This has continued in Britain to modern times; in 2015 a new twelve-sided coin – designed by a 15-year-old boy – was announced specifically to beat fraud.

Henry believed the coins, some of which still dated from Stephen's reign, had deteriorated badly, and he introduced a new standard coin, dubbed the 'Tealby penny' after a hoard found in Tealby, Lincolnshire in 1807. Initially, 30 mints were set the task of producing

Henry II

25 Kate Norgate, *England Under the Angevin Kings* (1887).

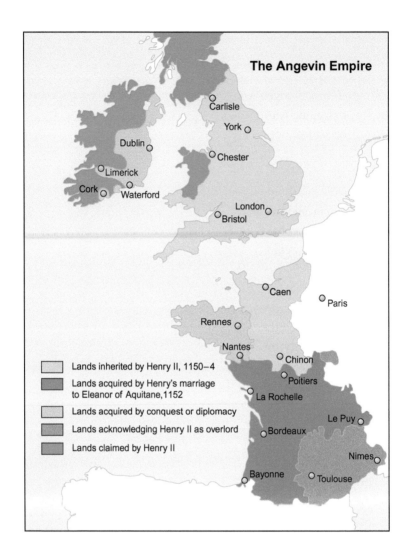

The Angevin Empire

- Carlisle
- York
- Dublin
- Chester
- Limerick
- Cork
- Waterford
- London
- Bristol
- Caen
- Paris
- Rennes
- Nantes
- Chinon
- Poitiers
- La Rochelle
- Le Puy
- Bordeaux
- Nimes
- Bayonne
- Toulouse

Lands inherited by Henry II, 1150–4

Lands acquired by Henry's marriage to Eleanor of Aquitane, 1152

Lands acquired by conquest or diplomacy

Lands acknowledging Henry II as overlord

Lands claimed by Henry II

the required coins; this number was later reduced to 12 mints which helped with quality control. However, the quality of the Tealby penny still did not satisfy Henry and a new style, the so-called short-cross penny, was introduced in 1180. It would survive until 1247, which not only gave confidence but demonstrated a new found stability in the country. The new sterling silver standard consisted of 92.5% silver and 7.5% copper.

However, Henry's vast 'empire' – he controlled more French territory than the King of France at one point, having married

Eleanor of Aquitaine – required close attention. Henry was a roving monarch, constantly on the move, spending just 17 months in England during the first eight years of his reign. He introduced the concept of circuit judges, who provided consistent rulings throughout the land, along with the juries of 12 knights, to reach impartial and fair decisions, but he also needed someone he could trust to watch his back while he was away and manage his affairs in England in his place. The obvious choice was his long-term friend, fellow bon viveur, and accomplished rider Thomas Becket. Thomas was his Lord Chancellor, and had served under the then Archbishop of Canterbury Theobald of Bec; it was Theobald who had recommended the highly efficient Thomas to the King as Lord Chancellor.

The power of the church as we have noted was all pervasive; it even had its own courts which had a tendency to hand down more lenient sentences than those of the Crown. This rankled with Henry, who felt there was too much crime in the country and saw an opportunity on Theobald's death to fix the problem. He offered the post of Archbishop of Canterbury to Thomas, his good friend, hunting partner, and drinking chum, whom he assumed would be certain to see things his way.

Thomas balked at the idea – he wasn't even a priest at that stage – and warned Henry that they would end up falling out. He wrote saying, 'Our friendship will turn to hate'. But Henry insisted. Becket was ordained a priest on 2 June 1162 and the next day consecrated Archbishop. But no sooner had Thomas become Archbishop than he changed, foreswore the good life, gave up fine food and wine, and even wore a hair shirt under his robes. He resisted Henry's demands and further angered him two years later by rejecting a new edict in the Constitution of Clarendon which called for less interference from the clergy, greater independence from Rome, and a ruling which allowed anyone found guilty by a church court to be punished by a royal court. Becket, like some of his predecessors, thought he should leave the country and seek safety in France.

On his return in 1170 he once again angered Henry by asking the Pope in Rome to excommunicate Roger de Pont L'Évêque, the Archbishop of York; Gilbert Foliot, the Bishop of London; and Josceline de Bohon, the Bishop of Salisbury, for crowning Henry the Young as the heir apparent, thereby usurping the authority of Canterbury. In a fury Henry made his disastrously misunderstood and regularly misquoted plea, 'Will no-one rid me of this turbulent priest?' However, the contemporary biographer Edward Grim says the words were: 'What miserable drones and traitors have I nourished and brought up in my household, who let their lord be treated with such shameful contempt by a low-born cleric?'

Whatever the precise words, the outcome was the same. Four knights took him at his word, rode to Canterbury, and killed Becket in the cathedral. Henry, overcome with remorse, walked barefoot through Canterbury, allowed himself to be flogged by the monks, and begged the Pope for forgiveness.

This is the best known story of Henry's reign but there was also a major innovation relevant to our story about coins. In effect, after 1180, Henry had taken back control of minting under royal authority and importantly recognised that England was a trading nation so some continuity of coinage was important. The constant re-coinages and demonetising of previous issues, typical until Henry's reign, did not help business on the Continent; after all, Henry had a major concern in ensuring his 'overseas' interests flourished. As a result of this stability, English coins became the common currency in northern Europe[26] – a novel thought in modern times as the pound sterling stands firmly against the Euro.

This continuity persisted into Richard I's (1189–1199) reign where coins inscribed HENRICUS REX were still in circulation. Maybe Richard just didn't care what the coins looked like – he only spent six months of his reign in England – so long as there were enough of them. Indeed, some coins struck in his name were French coins, such as one in his capacity as the Count of Poitiers, so it is the lack of coinage which tells the tale of his reign.

He would eventually ascend to the throne after long-running battles with his father and his brothers over land which Henry had promised to them. Henry made his eldest son, Henry the Younger, joint King and heir, and promised his sons territory, but he was not going to relinquish control of the revenues that the land delivered before his death. So, egged on by their mother,

26 Warren, *The Governance of Norman and Angevin England*.

Eleanor of Aquitaine, Henry the Younger, Geoffrey, and Richard, Eleanor's favourite, began campaigning against their father, largely in France. They had support from barons on both sides of the Channel as well as the blessing of Louis VII, who was still smarting having lost his wife, Eleanor, to Henry after their earlier marriage was declared void when they failed to have a son.

The youngest sibling, John, Henry's favourite, was left behind in England, but Henry must have wondered what sort of children he had produced as one by one they would turn against him.

However, with superior forces and infinitely greater financial resources, Henry II eventually defeated his sons and King Louis in battle, reaching a truce with Louis in 1174, the Treaty of Montlouis. The rebellious sons were sent round France punishing the very barons who had supported them, and Eleanor was held captive by Henry until his own death in 1189.

Before his father died, Richard rose up in rebellion once more, this time facing his own brothers as well, pausing only briefly on the death of Henry the Younger, which left Richard as the eldest son and therefore heir to the throne. In 1189, Richard allied himself with the new young King Philip II of France, pursuing his ageing father and eventually cornering him at Ballans in south-west France. Feeble and unable to resist, Henry submitted to Richard whispering in his ear, 'God grant that I do not die until I have avenged myself on you'. But it wasn't to be. As he lay on his deathbed in Chinon Castle he was shown a list of all who had betrayed him and at the top of the list was his favourite son, John. He is said to have uttered with his dying breath the words, 'Shame, shame on a conquered king'. When Richard looked down on his father blood ran from Henry's nostrils – a sign some say of the presence of a murderer. Henry was buried at nearby Fontevraud Abbey.

Richard ('the Lionheart') was first and foremost a warrior who regarded his kingdom in England as little more than a source of revenue, selling lands and titles to fund his battles, most notably answering the call to the Third Crusade against the Muslim Saladin whose forces had captured Jerusalem. So little regard did Richard seem to have for the unity of his kingdom that in the very year he was crowned, he agreed terms with William the Lion, under the so-called Quitclaim of Canterbury, releasing Scotland from its oath of allegiance to the King of England, imposed by the Treaty of Falaise. Richard accepted 10,000 marks from William in return for his approval, and promptly set off to the Holy Land the following summer.

While he did manage to raise the Siege of Acre, succeeding where Philip II of France had failed, he did not achieve the Crusade's primary goal to secure Jerusalem, and having reached an agreement with Saladin allowing Christians access to the city, he headed home to England. On his way back his ship was wrecked in the Adriatic, and as he continued across enemy lands into Austria, he was captured by Henry VI, the Holy Roman Emperor, who held him for 15 months demanding a ransom. He was eventually released after a steep 150,000 marks was paid, which hardly makes the Quitclaim sound like a good deal.

During his absence his brother, John, had set up an alternative court, taking advantage of the unpopularity of William Longchamp, the Bishop of Ely, whom Richard had made his Lord Chancellor to run state business in his absence with John as Regent. But John appointed his own Lord Chancellor and set about negotiating side deals with Philip, only succeeding in losing land in northern France.

In due time Richard made it back to England, forgave his brother for his youthful exuberance, but then spent the rest of his life fighting to restore the land that had been lost in France. He eventually died having been wounded by a crossbow arrow in April 1199 at the Siege of Chalus-Chabrol. He was buried in Fontevraud Abbey alongside his father who hated him and his mother who betrayed her husband. Although he had entered a probably loveless marriage to Berengeria of Navarre, they had no children, leaving the way for John (1199–1216) to ascend the throne.

History has been overly generous to Richard who, while being a courageous and able fighter, was profligate when it came to spending vast sums on war. At the same time it has been unkind to King John who, importantly for our story, was in fact an able administrator, which was useful, as like his brother, Richard, he needed large sums for his ongoing and ultimately fruitless campaigning in

France. Winston Churchill in his work, *A History of the English-Speaking Peoples*, wrote: '...the British nation and the English-speaking world owe far more to the vices of John than to the labours of virtuous sovereigns.'[27]

John's dwindling lands in France meant he needed to exert more pressure on the money-making machine he operated in England and Ireland. Apart from swingeing court fines, the imposition of scutage, which allowed for payments to be made in lieu of providing men to fight, even though there were fewer and fewer campaigns, he also imposed hefty fines on land barons. They were made to pay what amounted to inheritance tax on the death of the previous nobles for estates and castles, and he showed favour to some by allowing them to pay for high office; of course, that only meant that newly appointed sheriffs, for example, then tried to claw back their investments by demanding more taxes from the poor. These were the days of the legendary Robin Hood and the wicked Sheriff of Nottingham

One of the consequences of the heavy taxation was an increase in clipping of coins as people kept the silver themselves, leading to a general shortage, exacerbated by the demands of the King's campaign war chest. However, John showed his administrative ability by withdrawing the old coins, some of which still bore Henry II's name and issuing a new silver penny bearing his own name and his image in an unusual three-quarter profile. The new coins went someway to improving quality and availability, as well as helping to boost the royal coffers.[28]

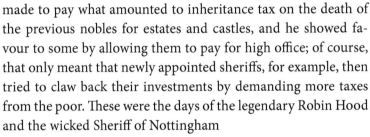

Penny, John

---

27 Winston Churchill, *A History of the English-Speaking Peoples*.
28 www.fitzmuseum.cam.ac.uk

THE ANGEVIN EMPIRE AND THE PLANTAGENETS

John also managed to raise considerable sums from the church when he fell out with Pope Innocent III over the appointment of a new archbishop of Canterbury. John wanted his own man, John de Gray, but Rome insisted on Stephen Langton. When the Pope went ahead and consecrated Langton in 1207 at a special ceremony in Rome, John refused to let him back into the country and seized the archbishopric lands as well as other papal property. John was excommunicated and England was placed under an interdict for five years (1208–1213); it was the severest of Church penalties, banning all ecclesiastical rites including baptisms, weddings, and burials in consecrated ground. John didn't mind as he earned an extra 100,000 marks in revenue from the property he had confiscated. In the end Archbishop Langton was accepted and John was allowed to keep all the money he had seized.

But, of course, it was John's financial squeezing of the barons, imposing heavy levies, bringing in more outsiders to positions of authority, and sometimes just pure venom towards those who fell out of favour because John felt they were a threat, which finally led to the revolt by the barons. For example, the unfortunate William de Braose was fined the equivalent of £26,666, an enormous sum in those days. When he could not pay, his wife and a son were imprisoned until their deaths, while de Braose sought exile until his own death in 1211.

Finally, in 1215, John was forced to put his seal on the Magna Carta at Runnymede, which among its rules granted people a right to be tried by their peers, and *habeas corpus*. No future king would simply be able to lock someone up on a whim.

As an aside, in 2015 when a new £2 coin was released celebrating 800 years since Magna Carta, the 'tails' side of the coin showed King John holding a quill apparently signing the document. A schoolboy error, historians cried, forcing the Royal Mint to release an explanation saying the image was only symbolic of the event and not to be taken literally. King John, of course, would not have signed anything; he would merely have applied his royal seal. Sometimes the stories coins tell us can be misleading.

At the time the Magna Carta did not bring about any lasting peace between John and the barons. Rebellion continued for the rest of his reign, not only with them but also with Llewelyn the Great in North Wales, Alexander II in Scotland, and even Prince Louis of France,[29] who had been invited to join the fray by the barons. He arrived unopposed and was even proclaimed King of England at St Paul's Cathedral, although he was not actually crowned, creating for a brief moment a dual monarchy.

By 1216 John was losing support and even lost the crown jewels and wagons filled with treasure as he tried to cross one of the estuaries in The Wash. But by now he had contracted dysentery and died on 18 October 1216, bringing an end to the Angevin line. It also sparked a change of heart among the barons, Louis lost his support, and under the terms of the Treaty of Lambeth, he agreed that he was never really the legitimate King of England, helped along with a 10,000 marks pay off.

It is appropriate to give a nod to Llewelyn the Great, who was the dominant leader of all Wales from 1216–1240, having struck deals with John and his successor, Henry III, and won the allegiance of the lesser princes around him. Although mints proliferated over the years in that country, Llewelyn does not appear to have issued any of his own coins, at least none that survives.

It is also right to mention the production of coins in Ireland during both John and Henry's reigns. The purpose of minting coins in Ireland struck from dies sent over from England was straightforward during John's reign: he needed the money for his campaigning in France. He had been made Lord of Ireland and paid his first visit in 1179. While he may have been conscientious in his duties there, he saw Ireland and its silver as a source of income as much as anything more noble. The quality of the silver in Ireland was the same as in England and the pennies in particular circulated freely in England as well as in Europe. Half

Penny, Henry III

29 Louis had a claim to the English throne by his marriage to Blanche of Castile, granddaughter of Henry II.

pennies and farthings were also struck, but most of these remained in Ireland as the practice of splitting whole pennies continued in England.[30] And as we shall see, Henry III (1216–1272) would also realise the benefit of Irish silver.

Henry was only nine years old when he ascended the throne, right in the middle of the First Barons' War, a struggle which would effectively continue throughout his reign, alongside his ongoing and expensive expeditions to secure and retain territories in France.

John knew he was going to die and arranged for a council of 13 executors to work with Henry under the leadership of William Marshall. The kingdom was in disarray. Half the country was in the hands of the rebel barons and John had lost Normandy, Brittany, Maine, and Anjou to Phillip II of France, leaving only Poitou and Gascony. John hoped his son would be able to win them back. The church stepped in and Cardinal Guala Bicchieri, the papal legate who had overseen Henry's coronation, declared that the young King was under the protection of the Pope in Rome and therefore the fight against the barons was nothing short of a crusade.

William Marshall's forces succeeded in defeating the rebels, who had been supported by Phillip's son, Prince Louis, at the decisive battle of Lincoln in 1217. When Louis returned later in the year and was defeated, he promised to try to persuade Phillip to return the French territory to Henry.

While William Marshall had been successful in seeing off the French, in the struggle with the rebel barons he was less successful. When the elderly William died, he was replaced at the head of the Government by Bishop Peter des Roches, who had actually crowned Henry; Hubert de Burgh, a former justiciar; and the new papal legate, Pandulf Masca. Gradually some order was restored, including a one-sided resolution in favour of Llewelyn in Wales, but once again there was trouble in France, as Louis took the opportunity of Henry's domestic weakness to attack Poitou and Gascony.

Henry desperately needed more money to bolster his under-resourced forces, and in 1225 a £40,000 tax was quickly raised

30 www.irishcoinage.com

to send an army into Gascony to retake the land. The following year Louis VIII died, bringing his 12-year-old son, Louis IX, to the French throne. If England had its divisions so too did France, as some of the nobles were loyal through their Angevin links to Henry. Some urged him to seize the opportunity of a new, underage King in France and attack.

Henry eventually began his campaigning in Poitou in 1230 but it was a disaster, and he returned to England having agreed a truce but little else. At home there was disagreement in court between the English under Hubert de Burgh and the Poitevin clique led by Bishop Peter des Roches. Hubert de Burgh lost the in-fighting and was imprisoned in the Tower of London.

Henry assumed personal responsibility for running affairs in 1234, dispensing with the great offices of state and instead relying on a council of trusted friends; for a time he appears to have been primarily concerned with uniting his English and French subjects. He married the 12-year-old Eleanor of Provence and Simon de Montfort, a French nobleman, married Henry's sister, also called Eleanor. He also devoted time and considerable sums of money to the arts and restoring and refurbishing his castles and houses, including Westminster Abbey.

So where was all the money coming from? A sizeable income was derived from Ireland where, in 1251, Henry re-opened the mint in Dublin for the striking of silver pennies; in style, Henry had replaced the long established short-cross pennies with a new long-cross design. Apart from anything else, the long cross on the reverse reaching to the edge of the coins made them harder to 'clip,' a process that reduced their weight and value. The new design also meant old mints had to be reopened. The Irish supply enabled him to export silver both to England and Europe, and during this time he built up stockpiles of gold. Henry needed the cash.

His Gascony adventures had cost him £200,000,[31] ruling out any hopes he may have had for going on a crusade to the Levant. The demands for money seem to be coming from every quarter: Pope Alexander IV wanted repayment for £90,000 squandered on

---

31 Huw W. Ridgeway, *Henry III (1207–1272)* (Oxford University Press, 2010).

supporting Henry's failed bid to win the crown of Sicily for his son, Edmund, from the Holy Roman Empire.

Not even Henry's treasure trove was enough to meet the demands, and it was not long before increased taxes sparked revolt in 1258 among the barons led by Henry's brother-in-law, Simon de Montfort. There was also rivalry among the French hangers-on in the royal court – Poitevins and Lusignans – who over the years had been shown favouritism by Henry. A compromise was reached under the Provisions of Oxford whereby Henry relinquished his personal rule, agreeing to work with a great council of barons who were able to appoint officials including the Lord Chancellor. Later, in 1259, a new set of rules – Provisions of Westminster – were agreed, placing restrictions on royal officials as well as curbing the power of some barons, although almost at once Henry began working behind the scenes to undermine the agreement, aided and abetted by Pope Urban IV.

Again the barons, led by de Montfort, rose up and managed to trap Henry and his wife Eleanor in the Tower of London, but they escaped and the unity among the barons faltered. The Second Barons' War erupted in April 1264 when Henry launched an attack on de Montfort's forces. They met at the Battle of Lewes, but despite having superior forces, Henry was defeated and he and his son, Edward, were captured. Effectively, de Montfort became the ruler of England, and sought to restore the terms of the Provisions of Oxford. He summoned the Great Parliament (1265), the first gathering of representatives from cities outside London, which would set a precedent for future generations and was the foundation of what would later become the House of Commons. Henry was forced to pardon the barons and for a while was King only in name.

However, Edward managed to escape, having been allowed to go hunting, and raised an army of his own, now supported by Gilbert de Clare, the Earl of Gloucester and de Montfort's most powerful ally at Lewes. At the Battle of Evesham in May that same year, Edward defeated de Montfort and released his father. De Montfort's body was mutilated and what was left was buried at Evesham Abbey, until Henry found out that it was becoming a place of pilgrimage and had the remains interred under a tree rather than in holy ground.

For the remaining years of his reign, Henry, who was growing frail, relied on Edward as steward of England. But the cupboard was bare, and in 1268, when Edward wanted to go on crusade himself, new taxes had to be raised. One twentieth of every citizen's possessions was demanded for the expedition. Not for the first time the pressure was put on the Jewish community to pay a large part of the bill. Jewish leaders were imprisoned on trumped-up charges and had to pay extortionate fines to win their release. During the regency the Jewish money lenders had flourished, but by 1253 Henry had passed the Statute of Jewry in an attempt to segregate the Jews and even enforce the wearing of Jewish badges. Indeed, as early as 1215 under one of the Canons of the Fourth Council of the Lateran, Pope Innocent III tried to insist that Jews as well as Muslims should wear distinctive clothes to set them apart from Christians. Canon 68 read in part:

> In some provinces a difference in dress distinguished the Jews or Saracens from the Christians, but in certain others such a confusion has grown up that they cannot be distinguished by any difference. Thus it happens at times that through error Christians have relations with the women of Jews or Saracens, and Jews and Saracens with Christian women. Therefore, that they may not, under pretext of error of this sort, excuse themselves in the future for the excesses of such prohibited intercourse, we decree that such Jews and Saracens of both sexes in every Christian province and at all times shall be marked off in the eyes of the public from other peoples through the character of their dress.[32]

And in 1218 England became the first European country to require Jews to wear badges. By 1290 Edward would order the expulsion of the Jews from England, and they would not return for more than 360 years.

Edward set off on the Eighth Crusade to the Holy Lands in 1270, ignoring his father's concerns that the barons might take advantage of his failing health and rebel again in his absence. But Edward's small force of 1,000 knights could do little on the Crusade apart from the relief of Acre and some small skirmishes. In June 1272, having survived an assassination attempt, he left for Sicily; his crusading days were over. Henry died in November and was buried in Westminster Abbey. When his body was exhumed in 1290 it was noted that it was in perfect condition, which some suggested meant he was a saint. However, he was never canonised and his heart was removed and buried in Fontevraud Abbey in Anjou alongside other members of his Angevin family; he may have been King of England but his heart was in France.

Edward I (1272–1307) was now King but did not reach England until the summer of 1274, which explains why coins continued to be minted in Henry's name even after his death. Henry left the nation poorer in terms of wealth and territory compared with the once expansive lands of the Angevin kings, and it would be up to Edward to try and sort matters out. He seemed to have all the necessary attributes for a strong medieval king: he was successful in battle, religious in manner, and a sound administrator, if something of a bully, even a bit of a tyrant according to some books. Despite all the strengths in his favour, money would remain a problem.

The epithet 'Hammer of the Scots' is enough to tell us that Edward's was an active reign, and activity in those days for a king invariably meant vast military expense, which even as heir to the throne he had wantonly enjoyed.

His first campaign was in Wales, where Llewelyn ap Gruffyd had not only taken advantage of the turmoil of the Barons' Wars in England and extended the land he controlled, but he had cocked a snook at Edward by not attending his coronation at Westminster. However, he was no match for the militarily seasoned Edward, who was able to deploy a vast force of 15,000 infantry and cavalry, as well as effectively use the navy along the North Wales coast. Having killed Llewelyn and his brother, David, and crushed all Welsh resistance, Edward then set about consolidating his victory by building a network of castles (e.g. Caernarvon and Harlech) at a further cost of some £80,000. For the first time the whole of Wales was under English rule and an English king. In 1284 Edward's son, also Edward, was born at Caernarvon and later became the first in a long line of English princes to be invested as Prince of Wales.

There was more campaigning to come in Scotland and France which all had to be paid for, but Edward was broke. He did this by summoning Parliament regularly to win backing for his policies, including imposing a uniformity of administration throughout the kingdom as well as authorising further taxation.

The penny, now 500 years old, was no longer adequate for business, and the quality of coins was still an issue. Both were improved with the introduction of three new denominations that appeared in England for the first time: the halfpenny, the farthing, which eliminated the old problem of clipping, and the groat, which was based on a French silver coin worth four English pennies. If you were spending money as fast as Edward was why not have a single coin worth four times as much as the existing coinage? Interestingly, the weight of the coins was not consistent, being regularly reduced to match the value of Continental coinage.

Penny, Edward I

The new coinage, of course, meant a charge could be made for exchanging all the old coins. The practice of including the moneyer's name was dropped but coins contained a privy mark showing slight variations in the King's appearance so the moneyer could be identified and presumably punished in the event of fraud. The production of dies was improved using engraving; the general format for the design of the coins would remain the same for the next 200 years. Indeed, new coins were not automatically minted on the accession of a new monarch; rather, they would have been produced purely for commercial reasons. As noted by the numismatists H. B. Earle Fox and John Shirley-Fox: 'How long actual coins of Edward I continued to circulate it is, perhaps, impossible to say, but they have certainly been found mixed with those of Henry VI.'[33]

Meanwhile, all had been well in Scotland until Alexander III died without a male heir – his two sons and daughter had predeceased him – leaving only Margaret of Norway, his granddaughter by his own daughter and King Eric II of Norway. In a suitably medieval arrangement by the Treaty of Birgham, it was decided that Margaret, aged seven, should marry Prince Edward, then aged just one. But Margaret died on the way to Scotland in 1290 and the succession developed into a crisis known as the Great Cause – only made worse for King Edward because his beloved wife, Eleanor, died the same year.

Many claimants to the Scottish crown came forward and Edward was asked to oversee the dispute, which he agreed to do, insisting that it should be accepted that he held 'sovereign lordship of Scotland and the right to determine our several pretensions.'[34]

Eventually, John Balliol was recognised as King, but Edward refused to give up his status as sovereign lord. Reluctantly, Balliol agreed, but when Edward also demanded that the Scots provide soldiers for his ongoing wars it was the last straw, and in alliance with the French who were at war with England over the Duchy of Gascony, the Scots attacked Carlisle. But they were no match for Edward. He defeated them and went on to exact revenge by invading Scotland in 1296, seizing the Stone of Destiny – the Scottish coronation stone – from Scone Abbey and taking it to Westminster Abbey, where it remained under the Coronation Chair until it was returned in 1996. Three Englishmen were appointed to run the country.

Crippling debt plagued Edward for the rest of his reign and resulted in his agreeing to constraints by Parliament. He was trying to fight on three fronts: in France, Wales, and Scotland. Peace was reached in France restoring Gascony to Edward, but he carried on campaigning in Scotland, where first William Wallace then Robert the Bruce rebelled. A fighter to the last, Edward headed north once more to take on Robert the Bruce after he crowned himself King of Scotland, but he died on his way there on 7 July 1307.

Edward II (1307–1327) had little to thank his father for when he came to the throne. He inherited huge debts, continuing trouble with rebellion in Scotland and Wales, the ongoing uncertainty over Gascony, and domestic problems with his own barons. Unfortunately, he did not possess any of the military or administrative skills of his father, and he compounded his difficulties by surrounding himself with a small clique of influential favourites, most notably Piers Gaveston, a Gascon, which angered the English nobility as well as the French royal family.

No sooner had Edward been proclaimed King then he summoned Gaveston, who may also have been his lover, from France to join his court. He also took the opportunity of dismissing and imprisoning Bishop Walter Langton from his post as Royal Treasurer (one of many treasurers he dismissed), no doubt in revenge for the Bishop's earlier complaints to Edward I about the Prince's extravagance.

When Edward left for France to marry King Philip IV's 12-year-old daughter, Isabella, in an attempt to secure peace between the two countries, he put Gaveston in charge as his *custos regni* in his absence – a guaranteed red rag to the barons. The coronation with his new bride on his return was another lavish affair, and even on this day Edward preferred the company of his friend rather than his queen. Matters came to a head in 1308 when Isabella (and the French monarchy) supported the barons in calling for Gaveston's removal; he was exiled, but only to Dublin with a new title, Lieutenant of Ireland.

In the meantime, Edward still had a problem with Robert the Bruce in Scotland, but he needed funds to launch a military campaign, which Parliament resisted until he agreed to a series of reforms. He made the concessions which got him his money and also opened the way to Gaveston's return. But his friend had not mellowed in the Irish air and returned to be just as abusive to the barons, many of whom refused to attend Parliament while he was still in the country.

Edward failed to raise an army and once again was back in Parliament asking for help while at the same time facing demands from the Frescobaldi bankers for repayment of a £22,000 outstanding loan. This time Edward was forced to agree to the appointment of 12 Ordainers tasked with reforming both the government and the royal household. Once more Edward headed north to confront Robert the Bruce, who simply withdrew into the mountains and watched while Edward's army ran out of supplies.

Apparently learning nothing and feeling threatened by the powerful nobles and their own armies, Edward revoked the Ordinances and brought Gaveston back, sparking fury among the barons who, led by Lancaster, effectively chased the King, his bride, and his friend out of London. Gaveston was eventually caught, found guilty of treason in what amounted to a kangaroo court headed by Lancaster, and executed.

Just when it looked liked another civil war would break out, a settlement was reached, and over the following months, Edward's precarious financial situation improved: Parliament agreed a new tax levy, he negotiated loans from his bankers and the Pope, and borrowed £33,000 from Philip of France.[35] For once he was flush with cash and ready to take on the Scots again.

In 1314, he headed north with some 20,000 soldiers to do battle with an emboldened Robert the Bruce who had just 6,000 men. The fateful meeting at Bannockburn is well-documented and been given the Hollywood spin in the film *Braveheart*, which focuses on William Wallace, although the 'brave heart' was actually that of Robert the Bruce, which would be carried into battle after his death. Edward just escaped with his life.

His failure on the battlefield was compounded by famine as the seemingly continuous rain between 1314 and 1321 destroyed harvests, while the cold winters killed the cattle. With some inevitability civil war broke out in 1321 between the Dispenser family, the King's new favourites who had grown wealthy under his patronage, and other nobles, among them the Earl of Lancaster. After various exchanges and switching of allegiances, Edward and

35 Seymour Phillips, *Edward II* (Yale University Press, 2011).

the Dispensers emerged victorious and Lancaster was executed. A series of summary trials were held around the country, where all of Edward's opponents were found guilty, many executed, and lands seized. The latter greatly enriched Edward, who soon found himself with a treasure trove of £62,000[36] – it was time to take on the Scots again.

In 1322, he moved north with an even larger army, but again Robert the Bruce simply vanished into the heather, and, unable to feed his soldiers, Edward was forced to withdraw. It was the third time he had been made to retreat by the Scots. Eventually a treaty was reached, much to Edward's annoyance, recognising Robert the Bruce as King of Scotland.

This still left the little matter of Gascony, which had blown up again with the arrival of Isabella's brother, Charles, as the new King of France. He demanded that Edward should come and pay him due homage as his overlord in the country. Edward responded by among other things seizing English property owned by the French including Isabella's land on the basis that she too was French.

Another war was not an option as funds were short again, so Edward sent Isabella, hardly a neutral arbitrator at this point, to negotiate terms on his behalf in March 1325. She cut a deal but it was very much in her brother's favour, still requiring Edward to pay homage. Then, instead of returning to England, she decided to stay in France because she disliked the way the Dispenser family behaved and held so much sway over her husband, and she was still smarting over the seizure of her land. But above all, Edward had taken Isabella's children and placed them in the custody of the Dispenser family.[37] Even the ruse of making his son, Edward, Duke of Gascony so he could pay homage to Charles in his stead did not work.

Isabella had also found a new paramour in France, the exiled Roger, Lord Mortimer, and she had no intention of returning unless it was at the head of a large invasion force of other disgruntled barons. That force also had the support of William, the Count of

36 Phillips, *Edward II*.
37 Paul Doherty, *Isabella and the Strange Death of Edward II* (London: Robinson, 2004).

Hainault, in the Low Countries, whose daughter, Philippa, had become betrothed to the 12-year-old Edward, heir to the English throne. William offered a fleet of vessels and warships as part of the dowry and Isabella made ready to invade.

Across the Channel, Edward himself had little support and little money. The Dispensers were loathed, and when the call went up to defend England, few people showed up, and mobs in London went on the rampage releasing any prisoners they found in the Tower of London.

Edward and his loyal Dispensers fled. Hugh Dispenser the Elder was soon caught and executed. When Edward and Hugh Dispenser the Younger tried to escape to Ireland bad weather forced them back and they were betrayed. Dispenser was found guilty of treason and sentenced to be hanged, drawn, and quartered. Edward agreed to abdicate while being held at Kenilworth Castle in favour of his son, Edward III (1327–1377).

Plots and rumours circulated about trying to restore Edward II to the throne and he was moved from castle to castle until his son was eventually told that his father had died at Berkeley Castle in mysterious circumstances.

But this is a story about money, and while Edward and his predecessors had struggled to fund their various campaigns, Isabella and Mortimer over-reached themselves as they ruled on behalf of the young Edward, who was only 14 when he ascended the throne. They made a deal with the Scots at the Treaty of Northampton by which, in return for £100,000, England would, among other conditions, recognise Robert the Bruce and all his heirs as rightful kings of an independent Scotland. The couple also grew immensely wealthy in their stewardship of the kingdom, and soon the muttering began.

Edward III, who had grown to dislike Mortimer, had them both arrested at Nottingham Castle in 1330. Mortimer was accused of murdering Edward II and executed while Isabella was spared. All the problems of Edward II's reign were heaped on Mortimer as the medieval spin doctors sought to change his image. The King's body was embalmed and buried at Gloucester Abbey (later Cathedral) where miracles were claimed.

Edward was a pragmatist as well as an able soldier. Rather than try to face a war on two fronts with the Scots and the French he reached an uneasy truce with David II in 1338 and focused his attention across the Channel, beginning by declaring himself as the rightful King of France as grandson of Philip IV. Invoking Salic law, the French rejected Edward's claim, recognising Philip VI as King. The Hundred Years War was underway.

At first Edward tried to make progress through political alliances, but these proved costly as well as ineffective, and the regency council began to complain about the rising national debt.

Edward switched tactics, favouring warfare to diplomacy, and in 1339 invaded France, sweeping through Brittany and Normandy, before defeating Philip at the Battle of Crécy in 1346. It was a decisive battle in many ways, changing military tactics learned as a result of fighting in Scotland, with greater use of mobile infantry against the heavily armoured knights and the use of the longbow and first deployment of cannon fire.

At home, an English army had defeated and captured David II of Scotland, who had risen up again, so now Edward could focus all his efforts on France, amassing a 35,000 strong army which eventually captured Calais in 1347 after nearly a year-long siege.

The following year the Black Death broke out, forcing a pause in hostilities which were not resumed until the 1350s. In 1356, Edward's eldest son, Edward the Black Prince, defeated the French at the Battle of Poitiers, capturing John II, the new French King, and thereafter there was desultory action until eventually the Treaty of Brétigny was signed in 1360. Edward renounced his claims to the French throne, but was granted large tracts of south-west France. John was released on payment of a mighty three million gold crowns along with two of his sons as hostages to secure the full payment. When one of the sons, Louis I, Duke of Anjou, escaped John gave himself up and eventually died in captivity.

The development of Edward as he grew into his monarchy is clearly traced in the coinage produced over the years. The first

coins Edward had minted were similar to the pennies of Edward I and II. He also introduced new denominations including the helm and the leopard but they were soon dropped. New gold coins – the noble, half noble and quarter noble – then appeared, and between 1344 and 1351 the first florin was minted – so-called because the dies were made by moneyers from Florence. The noble was the most valuable coin in England. Most notably, immediately after the Treaty, coins were inscribed: EDWARD R ANGL FRANC, EDWARDUS REX ANGLIE FR, EDWARD REX ANGL FR – 'Edward King of England and France'; an overly ambitious claim, although briefly after Brétigny the claim to France was dropped as new coins were minted.

Leopard design, Edward III

While English and Scottish kings seem to have been continuously at war with each other, until 1373 Scottish coins were regularly used in England and had the same values. At the time, with England controlling much of the border countries, Robert II, the first King of the Royal House of Stewart, allowed his earls to try to win back the territory, trade with England was halted, and closer ties with France pursued. The reality was that Robert was elderly by medieval standards and struggled to control his earls.

Groat, Robert II

Charles V succeeded John as King of France, and claiming that Edward had broken the terms of the Treaty of Brétigny, declared war; after a nine year break the Hundred Years War was on again. But this time Edward, or rather his sons, who increasingly did most of the fighting on his behalf, was less successful. This lack of victory, and most importantly the cost of waging war, once again proved unpopular with the English Parliament, which insisted Edward proved the necessity of more campaigning. French territory was being lost and Edward's closest advisers were dying through old age or a recurrence of the Black Death.

John of Gaunt, Edward's third surviving son, was no match for an increasingly powerful Parliament, which gradually developed into the two chamber system we have today. In 1376, the so-called 'Good Parliament' only agreed to further taxation in return for concessions from the Crown including the dismissal of a number of his advisers and the banishment from court of Alice Perrers, the King's mistress, who was said to be having a malign influence over him. Parliament was beginning to get the upper hand over the Crown.

The following year Edward died and was succeeded by his ten-year-old grandson, Richard II (1377–1399), son of the Black Prince who had died the previous year after a prolonged illness having contracted dysentery, so often the killer illness of the time, while fighting in Spain.

There was no challenge to Richard's claim to the throne, which may explain why he appears to have been in no hurry to order the minting of new coins – the existing coinage (pennies, groats, farthings etc.) in his father's name was plentiful and acceptable for commerce. He did later strike his own coins but he did not have a point to make about his right to the throne so there was no urgency. That would come later with his successor.

Penny, Richard I

For most of Richard's reign, he would persist in claiming the French throne but without any military success in the Hundred Years War, which was still rumbling on. Taxation to foot the bill was increasingly resented and it was not long before there was a general uprising, the Peasants' Revolt, in 1381. The rebels, led by Wat Tyler, marched on London, demanding a reduction in taxation and an end to serfdom. After initial setbacks for the King – many of his troops were fighting on the Continent – at just 14 years of age, he agreed to meet the rebels and accepted their terms. It was a short lived victory because when sufficient forces were organised, the rebel leaders were rounded up and executed, and the concessions granted by the King were rescinded on the advice of the royal council – Lords Appellant – who were essentially the Government, which in itself caused ill-feeling with Parliament.

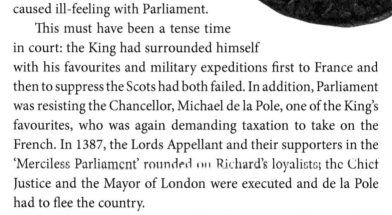

This must have been a tense time in court: the King had surrounded himself with his favourites and military expeditions first to France and then to suppress the Scots had both failed. In addition, Parliament was resisting the Chancellor, Michael de la Pole, one of the King's favourites, who was again demanding taxation to take on the French. In 1387, the Lords Appellant and their supporters in the 'Merciless Parliament' rounded on Richard's loyalists; the Chief Justice and the Mayor of London were executed and de la Pole had to flee the country.

For the next few years Richard seems to have worked alongside the Lords Appellant, but in 1397 he asserted himself and began to take revenge – Richard's 'tyranny' – and had many of them executed or forced into exile. Although his uncle, John of Gaunt, Duke of Lancaster, was not one of the principal advisers, as nominal Regent to the young King he was regarded as influential and his family potentially a threat. So on John's death in 1399, Richard disinherited John's son, Henry Bolingbroke, who had been banished to France, and divided up the powerful Duchy of Lancaster among his friends.

Henry IV

In June the same year, Bolingbroke landed in England initially aiming to regain his land only to find little resistance; indeed he attracted widespread support. Richard was away in Ireland and did not return until July, landing in Wales. When the King arrived he was met by the Duke of Northumberland and arrested. One-sided negotiations followed and in September he abdicated. Bolingbroke claimed the throne as male heir through his father, John of Gaunt, Edward's third son, and swiftly had himself crowned Henry IV (1399–1413) the next month, making the first public address in English since William the Conqueror.

Meanwhile, Richard was held prisoner until his death in 1400, possibly starved to death in Pontefract Castle, although rumours persisted that he actually survived for another 19 years in Scotland.

5 THE LANCASTRIANS AND THE YORKISTS

1399–1485

Henry's mother, Blanche, had inherited the estates of her father, the Duke of Lancaster, the wealthiest peer in the land, ushering in the Lancastrian line; but wealth has never been a guarantee of stability, and it wasn't for her son.

Henry had usurped the throne and felt vulnerable. To press home his claim of legitimacy as King, he immediately had new coins struck in his name. On the obverse of the groat was written HENRIC DI GRA REX ANGLE Z FRACIE ('Henry by the grace of God King of England and France'), while some read HENRIC DI GRA REX ANGL Z DNS HIBS Z AQ to include Ireland and specifically Aquitaine. Clearly, France was still high on the royal agenda as the Hundred Years War continued.

The quality of the coinage was inferior – a handy metaphor perhaps for his reign. The old practice of merchants from the Continent melting down the high-quality English silver coins and returning with debased silver coins mixed with tin, lead, and copper continued. So although Henry controlled the mints in London, York, and Durham, bullion was slipping away, and as ever, the military campaigns cost money.

He may have felt the new coinage made him legitimate, but his reign was plagued by rebellion and would ultimately lead to all-out civil war. The death, or murder, of Richard finally put paid to any threat of his return to power, with Henry successfully seeing off the so-called Epiphany Rising in 1400 among conspirators who wanted to restore Richard to the throne.

In the same year, Henry found himself having to deal with the seemingly age-old problem of rebellion in Wales. Owen Glendower was an experienced soldier who had served under John of Gaunt for Richard II in his battles with the Scots and took part in the defeat of the French, Spanish, and Flemish fleet in the Channel in 1387. Later, he may also have served alongside Henry, before he became King, at the Battle of Radcot Bridge in the same year against troops loyal to Richard II. So he was a seasoned campaigner. He was also the least likely rebel, being comfortably off, well-educated, and well-connected with English high society – his patron was the powerful Richard Fitzalan, Earl of Arundel.

However, in what amounted to a land grab, his neighbour, Baron Grey de Ruthyn, seized some of Glendower's property. Glendower appealed to the English Parliament for redress but it ruled in the Baron's favour. It was just another example in Welsh eyes that they were being discriminated against in their own country. Key posts were being filled by the English, taxation by the English Parliament was punitive, and even jobs were scarce; the whispering in Glendower's ear was telling him that enough was enough and that he was the man to sort the problems out. The Welsh Revolt was about to begin.

Glendower declared himself Prince of Powys, and when the Penal Laws against Wales were passed in 1402 banning the Welsh from holding high office, bearing arms, or even buying property in English towns, the floodgates opened. Welsh workers in England left their jobs and battle hardened soldiers of Welsh descent deserted to serve under Glendower in a series of skirmishes, while Welsh students abandoned their studies to take up arms. In 1404 Glendower held his own first Parliament and proclaimed himself Prince of Wales. The following year he signed a treaty with the French who saw an opportunity to be rid of the claimant to their throne. But it was all bluster, and by 1406 the mood in France had shifted to peace under a new King, Charles VI, while the English adopted different military tactics, cutting off Glendower's supplies. Gradually his castles fell while he himself slipped away and was never seen again.

Meanwhile, Henry had to see off a rebellion led by the Archbishop of York, Richard Le Scrope, and the Earl of Northumberland, followed by a second uprising by the Earl in northern England, backed by the Scots in 1408. Northumberland was killed at the Battle of Bramham Moor.

In the final years of his reign, Henry was not a well man, suffering either from psoriasis, epilepsy, or even leprosy depending on the account one believes. The leprosy legend suggests it was inflicted on him by God for having the Archbishop of York executed following his failed uprising.

Henry V (1413–1422) in his short but eventful reign managed to unite most of the fragmented loyalties at home which left him free to pursue the never-ending claim to the French crown. While his coins were largely similar to his father's, some omit the reference to Aquitaine, presumably to make the point that the whole of France was considered part of the kingdom. The mints were kept busy although Henry tried to maintain standards by introducing mint marks on the coins.

In 1415, Henry arrived in France, took Harfleur and marched on Calais, meeting the French knights on the plains of Agincourt in October. The heavens opened and the heavily armoured French, bogged down in the mud, were easy prey for the English archers, although much of the fighting was hand-to-hand combat with the English using hammers and axes against armoured men struggling in heavy ground already churned up by horses. Henry pressed home his advantage, took Rouen, and by August 1419 had reached Paris, which capitulated.

The following year the Treaty of Troyes was signed, recognising Henry and any sons as the rightful heirs to the French throne upon the death of Charles VI. The treaty also arranged the marriage of Henry to Catherine of Valois, Charles's daughter. In the event, Charles outlived Henry, who died in 1422, possibly from dysentery, aged just 36.

Henry's sudden death left the succession vulnerable once again as his son, Henry VI (1422–1461), was only nine months old at the time. Before he died Henry had appointed his brother, John, Duke of Bedford, as Regent of France, and John's younger brother, Humphrey, Duke of Gloucester, became Lord Protector of England. Conflict for overall control of the kingdom was inevitable.

Henry VI also became King of France on the death just weeks later of his maternal grandfather, Charles VI, under the terms of the Treaty of Troyes, and continued to control most of northern France until 1453, although control was certainly not in his hands. At the start of his reign the appointed regents ran the kingdom, and when he eventually married at the age of 16, his own easy-going character and bouts of insanity meant his future wife, Margaret of Anjou, would be the actual ruler. It was to be a long, unhappy reign, and civil war was not far off.

By the time Henry assumed control in 1437 when he was 16 the Hundred Years War had stalled as far as England was concerned; Joan of Arc was winning a series of battles and some sort of diplomacy looked a better option. Henry was inclined to find a peaceful solution backed by Cardinal Henry Beaufort, Bishop of Winchester, and William de la Pole, Earl of Suffolk. Those in favour of fighting on were Humphrey, Duke of Gloucester, and Richard, Duke of York. But, to cement peaceful relations, Henry agreed to marry the beautiful Margaret of Anjou, niece of the 'rival' King of France, Charles VII.

The marriage went ahead in 1445 when Margaret turned 15, but secretly, under the Treaty of Tours, it had been agreed that England would give up claims to Maine and Anjou. By the time the terms of the deal leaked out the wedding had taken place, but Gloucester and York were furious and they directed their anger at Suffolk.

However, determined to protect their man and probably at Margaret's instigation, charges of treason were brought against Gloucester who died – possibly poisoned – before he could be brought to trial, while York, great-grandson of Edward III, Prince of Wales, and by agreement with Henry his heir, was sent to Ireland. He was clearly seen as a threat to the king.

The problem was that between them, Henry, Margaret, and a court full of their favourites were incapable of running the country. Law and order was breaking down, corruption was rife, and the economy was a shambles; even the soldiers who had been fighting in France had not been paid. The value of Henry's reputation, as well as his coins, was severely devalued. The Duke of Suffolk was impeached by Parliament, and was caught and killed when he tried to flee across the Channel.

In 1453, Henry suffered another mental breakdown and the Duke of York was summoned back to England to take over as Regent, restore order, and balance the books;[38] the Queen was completely side-lined.

The following year, Henry appeared to have recovered and for a time it was agreed that Richard, Duke of York, should succeed him. But, after numerous minor exchanges, the first major battle in what would later become known as the Wars of the Roses was fought at St Albans in 1455. A brief period of peace followed before renewed fighting broke out in 1459. York was forced to flee but one of his supporters brought troops over from Calais and captured Henry at the Battle of Northampton.

Thereafter fortunes swung back and forth. The Lancastrians decisively won the Battle of Wakefield where York and one of his sons were killed, and at the Second Battle of St Albans the royalists managed to release Henry but failed to capitalise on their success and take London. York's eldest son was proclaimed Edward IV (1461–1470 and 1471–1483). Once again such was the tenuous hold on the throne that we see coins quickly struck in Edward's name.

Fighting between the two camps continued, and in 1464, Henry was recaptured. But Edward fell out with his supporters, notably the Earl of Warwick, dubbed the 'Kingmaker', who plotted to have Henry restored to the throne. However, Edward had two important victories – Barnet and Tewkesbury – and the tables were turned once again. Henry was murdered

Edward IV

38 Ralph Griffiths, *The Reign of Henry VI* (Berkeley: University of California Press, 1981).

in the Tower of London, bringing an end to the Lancastrian line.

Edward lavished titles and estates on his brother, Richard, Duke of Gloucester, who established a power base in the north of England. When Edward died suddenly in 1483, Richard quickly stepped in to run the country while his nephew, Edward V (1483), was still a minor, having been appointed as Lord Protector of England by Edward on his deathbed. The young Edward and his brother, Richard of Shrewsbury, Duke of York, were kept under 'close protection' in the Tower of London before Edward's coronation. But, in what amounted to a medieval spin campaign, Edward IV's marriage to Elizabeth Woodville was declared invalid and as a consequence their children illegitimate. As a result Edward was deemed no longer eligible to be King, he was never crowned, and he and his brother were never seen again. Known forevermore as the 'Princes in the Tower,' their deaths have always been widely attributed to their uncle, Richard, who promptly declared himself King Richard III (1483–1485), claiming the throne through his parents, Richard Plantagenet, Duke of York, and Cecily Neville.

Although Edward 'reigned' for just 86 days coins were struck in his name, and of course, Richard was quick to stamp his legitimacy on the throne with coins such as the groat marked RICARDVS DI GRA REX ANGLI Z FRANC ('Richard by the grace of God, King of England and France') – persisting with the claim over

Silver groat of Edward V

France – when he was crowned. Many of his coins were struck in York, where he had a strong supporter base, by the Archbishop Thomas Rotherham, marked with a 'T' and a key either side of the King's head. But since the value of the coins was in their silver content, as the price of the metal increased, the size and thickness of the coins decreased and they became very thin and consequently today are very rare.[39]

Richard's short reign combined with the notoriety of his ascendancy to the throne make his coins both scarce and valuable as investments. The most valuable are the angel and half angel. Recently the discovery of his remains under the ruins of Grey Friar's Chapel under a car park in Leicester, and subsequent reburial with all due pomp at Leicester Cathedral in 2015, captured the public's imagination. Crowds gathered, some holding the white York rose, to watch his funeral cortege complete with mounted knight in armour, apparently suspending in their minds the stories/rumours swirling round about his life. Was he complicit in the Princes' murder? Had he in fact been maligned? Had he only acted to defend the realm as Lord Protector from the manoeuvring of the late King's widow and family? Indeed was he even really hunchbacked, as portrayed by Shakespeare and others, or just suffering from a bone disorder easily concealed by clothes?

The facts of his actual reign are not disputed. No sooner had he seized the throne than his support started ebbing away, at first falteringly with a failed rebellion led by the Duke of Buckingham when some of his supporters jumped the gun by rising up too soon; Buckingham was betrayed and executed. And then, in August 1485, after months of preparation, Henry Tudor, Earl of Richmond, a Lancastrian claimant to the throne who had spent much of his childhood in Brittany for his own protection from Richard, landed at Milford Haven in South Wales. He marched through the country picking up supporters and deserters from Richard's cause to confront the King's army at Bosworth Field. Richard had a superior force but was fatally compromised when

39 www.numsoc.net

Sir John Stanley changed sides and went into battle against the King in support of his step-nephew, Henry.

Richard was killed, some say by Welsh landowner Rhys ap Thomas by a blow to the head with a poleaxe, making him the last king to die in battle on English soil and bringing an end to the Yorkist line.

Nearly ninety years of fighting, intrigue, betrayal, and murder had not left the nation in a healthy state. As reflected in its coins, so thin and diminished in the end that they are a rarity, what was needed was a period of calm, stability, and unity. The Wars of the Roses were not entirely over; skirmishes continued and the new King's claim to the throne was about as thin as the coinage of the realm, but it needed to work.

6 THE TUDOR DYNASTY

From an economic point of view, the arrival of Henry VII (1485–1509) was vitally important to the country, which had been wracked by a combination of civil war and endless fruitless expeditions to win territory in France, not to mention the impact of the Black Death on the population. England's trade with the Continent had dried up, there were fewer workers, and the country was in a recession. What was urgently needed above all was a period of peace. It is worth mentioning as an aside that while Britain and Europe were flailing around, scholars in the Middle East and beyond were making great strides in medicine, mathematics, and developing altogether more civilised pursuits. Militarily and politically the Ottoman Empire (1299–1923) was rising to the height of its power and influence, particularly under the Sultanate of Suleiman the Magnificent (1520–1566), and the domestic squabbles between England and France must have seemed inconsequential.

As a distant relative of the Lancastrian kings, Henry's claim to the throne was tenuous at best, , but he had defeated Richard in war and he honoured his long standing commitment to marry Elizabeth of York, daughter of Edward IV, thereby uniting the two houses; they were third cousins as great-great-grandchildren of John of Gaunt. It also brought an end to the Wars of the Roses, symbolically combining the red rose of Lancaster and the white rose of York in his heraldic emblem, the Tudor Rose.

Sporadic rebellion continued throughout the reign as claimants to be rightful heirs to the throne emerged with their sponsors. In 1487, Lambert Simnel was championed by disaffected Yorkists, claiming to be son of Edward IV's brother, Clarence, but the rebellion was defeated and the young Simnel, regarded as an innocent puppet in the plot, was given a job in Henry's kitchens.

Three years later a Fleming, Perkin Warbeck, claimed to be Richard, son of Edward IV and one of the Princes in the Tower, and managed to garner support for his cause from France and the Netherlands. But Henry had no intention of getting into another overseas adventure and quickly persuaded the Netherlands to abandon their support of Warbeck. By the signing of a treaty, the *Magnus Intercursus*, in 1496 peace was restored, and even more importantly, trade with the Continent increased. Two years earlier Henry had imposed a trade embargo with the Netherlands, and Flemish traders had been thrown out of the country; the squeeze worked, and as a result of the Treaty, English merchants enjoyed favourable taxation terms with the Continent; this was part and parcel of Henry's desire to encourage English merchants to travel far and wide to discover new lands. This after all was a time when the Crown of Castile, a state on the Iberian Peninsula, and Portugal were looking to wider horizons; in 1494 by the Treaty of Tordesillas the world had been ambitiously divided between the two countries and even sanctioned by the Pope in Rome, although there was plenty of disagreement about where the dividing lines should fall.

Above all, Henry wanted to accumulate funds into the Royal Treasury to give him some independence from Parliament, and he achieved this in part by having consistency in his financial advisers; for most of his reign he only had two Lord High Treasurers: Lord Dynham and Thomas Howard, Earl of Surrey.[40] His Chancellor, Archbishop John Morton, also devised a way of increasing taxes from the nobles creating the 'Morton's Fork': those who spent little must have saved a great deal and those who spent a lot must have money to burn – either way, they could afford to pay higher taxes. An elegant 'Catch 22'.

Ever alert to a good deal Henry also became involved in the trading of alum used in the dyeing of cloths by licensing ships and acted as a go-between with suppliers in the Ottoman Empire and buyers in the Low Countries – it was a lucrative sideline for the King.[41] He also hoped to enjoy whatever riches merchant

---

40 S.B. Chrimes. *Henry VII* (Yale University Press, 1999).
41 Thomas Penn, *Winter King – Henry VII and the Dawn of Tudor England* (Simon & Schuster, 2013).

adventurers like John Cabot discovered in their travels replicating, he hoped, the success of Christopher Columbus. When Cabot set off in search of the treasures said to await them in Asia, Henry magnanimously granted Cabot the right to govern any new lands he discovered and to trade duty-free with England, only having to pay Henry a fifth of 'the Capital so gotten'.[42] Alas, Cabot only reached America and never returned; presumably, he drowned.

While the King may have been making money through taxes and customs duties on the increased trade, the average labourer would have made just £5 per year, while a nobleman could probably earn up to £3,000 per year. For the most part people traded in pennies and groats, all with varying mint marks including, of course, the rose, as well as a leopard, greyhound, anchor, and pansy. The first pound coin – the sovereign – appeared in 1489.

Henry was happy to encourage trade but he was less happy about the influx of inferior quality coinage from the Continent, and in 1498, issued a Proclamation Against Roman Coins in a vain attempt to ban groats and half goats issued by the Holy Roman Emperor, as well as substandard Irish pennies,[43] all of which were underweight and had been illegally used to deal with the shortage of domestic coins.

Above all, Henry restored order in a country where overly powerful barons could easily have proved to be a problem. His Star Chamber delivered swift justice; it cut through red tape and was designed to bolster the work of his justices of the peace, who may have been intimidated by the nobles. Fines were imposed if those nobles broke laws, effectively banning private armies.

Henry's eldest son, Arthur, died in 1502 leaving his brother, Henry, as next in line to the throne. When Henry VII eventually died at Richmond Palace, he bequeathed his son a realm in sound financial health with a Treasury full of money. He had also restored order by successfully keeping the barons in their place, eliminated any potential rivals to the throne, and introduced a sound judicial system.

---

42 James Evans , *Merchant Adventurers* (Phoenix, 2013); James Williamson, *The Cabot Voyages and Bristol Discovery Under Henry VII* (Cambridge University Press, 1962)

43 Glyn Davies, *A History of Money* (University of Wales Press, 2010)

It all started so well for Henry VIII (1509–1547). He had the looks and he had the fortune – the equivalent of about £375 million in today's money – but both would be lost well before the end of his reign. Accident and extravagance appear to have been the root causes of his physical decline coupled, of course, with an overwhelming desire to leave behind a son and heir, which led to his split with Rome.

Henry VIII

The accident was a fall while jousting, one of his favourite pastimes, which not only left him unconscious for a time, but also inflicted a wound which never properly healed. As he was no longer able to pursue his physical interests, including real tennis and hunting, his appetite would eventually result in the figure we have become familiar with in Hans Holbein paintings; an impressive but overweight man probably suffering from what we now call Type 2 diabetes, as well as suppurating leg wounds.

But before his body failed him, Henry displayed intellect and energy. He could speak Latin, French, and some Italian; he wrote books and poetry and was an accomplished musician, skilled at the lute, organ, and virginal. He composed music – although probably not the ballad/poem *Greensleeves*, despite popular legend – and wrote books, among them was *Assertio Septem Sacramentorum* ('Defence of the Seven Sacraments') in 1521, for which Pope Leo X bestowed on him the title *Fidei Defensor* ('Defender of the Faith'). The work defended the sacramental nature of marriage and supremacy of the Pope in Rome, both of which Henry, of course, would challenge; to this day the inscription FID, DEF, or FD appears on every coin – it is just a question of which faith. Prince Charles, the Prince of Wales, has indicated that when he becomes King he would like to be known as Defender of Faith, a subtle but profound difference which he believes will help unite society in a diverse and multi-cultural Britain.

Henry VIII

Where Henry's father had been modest in his spending, the young King was extravagant in his decoration of palaces and in his collection of exotic weapons. But it was in war and in particular the continuing claim to France which proved so costly. The reverse of his gold crown minted c.1544–1547 shows the arms of England and France.

Henry's brother, Arthur, died aged just 15, by which time he was already married to Catherine of Aragon, daughter of King Ferdinand II of Aragon and Queen Isabella I of Castile. Henry himself was still only 10 but in the political niceties of the time there was no objection to an arrangement being made for his marriage to his brother's widow if it meant keeping relations between England and Spain secure. The betrothal was approved and received the papal blessing, but by the time Henry reached 14 he thought better of the engagement and refused to go ahead with the marriage.

However, two months after his father's death, Henry changed his mind, and after a low-key wedding ceremony, he took his bride to their coronation in Westminster Abbey where no expense was spared. But it was the first of six unsatisfactory marriages.

Catherine gave birth to a still-born girl, followed by a son who survived just seven weeks. She miscarried again and then in 1516 their daughter, Mary was born. Henry bore no real ill will towards Catherine, but he still yearned for a son.

Meanwhile, he was trying to maintain a balancing act of friendship with both Louis XII of France and Ferdinand of Spain, but it wasn't to last, and in 1513, Henry invaded France with mixed results. First, the English navy was defeated at Brest, but then Henry returned with more support and captured Tournai in northern France. Overall it produced little and cost a great deal. Henry's war chest was running low and he had to turn to Parliament to sanction more expenditure. While he had been away Queen Catherine had seen off an opportunistic attack by James IV of Scotland at the Battle of Flodden in which James himself had been killed; although she had been successful, it was another costly affair.

Working behind the scenes throughout this period was the redoubtable Thomas Wolsey, Henry's almoner or Keeper of the Privy Purse. It was he who arranged for Henry's 18-year-old sister, Mary Tudor, to marry the 52-year-old Louis XII of France to restore relations between the two countries, even though Louis was dead within a year of the wedding. Although Catherine may have disapproved because it distanced England from Spain, Henry was more than happy with the arrangement and appointed Wolsey his Lord Chancellor.

In 1520, anxious about the deteriorating relations between the Emperor Charles V and the new King of France, Francis I, Henry got Wolsey to arrange a sumptuous gathering of jousting and partying which lasted two weeks, as depicted in the painting *The Field of the Cloth of Gold*,[44] in order to bring about a 'universal peace'. Although sanctioned by Henry, the elaborate event was undoubtedly Wolsey's doing. He was the real ruler of the country between 1514 and 1529, and enjoyed the trappings of success, living in style at Hampton Court Palace, freeing Henry to indulge in his hunting. Wolsey had his own agenda; he hoped that by backing Charles, the Emperor would support him in his bid to become Pope. In the event Charles did not need English support, as in 1525, he defeated and captured Francis at the Battle of Pavia, a decisive exchange in the Italian Wars. Charles went on to sack Rome two years later placing Pope Clement VII, who had supported the French, under his control.

None of this helped Henry or his Chancellor, who was beginning to lose his diplomatic touch, as it left England isolated

---

44 Attributed to various artists including Hans Holbein but probably the work of several painters c.1550.

having backed the wrong horse by siding with France. Henry, whose his eyes had alighted on Anne Boleyn, still needed a son, and Wolsey could not succeed in getting his marriage annulled by the Pope who was accountable to the Emperor Charles. The King would have to take matters into his own hands.

He sacked his Chancellor, who died on his way to face trial, replaced him with Sir Thomas More, and installed Thomas Cranmer as the new Archbishop of Canterbury. Cranmer immediately declared the King's marriage to Catherine null and void, leaving the way clear for Henry to marry Anne Boleyn, who was already pregnant. The consequence, of course, changed the development of British history, leading to the Reformation and establishment of the Church of England.

In 1534, by the Act of Supremacy, Henry was declared head of the Church of England with no right of appeal to Rome on ecclesiastical matters, leaving Pope Clement no choice but to excommunicate him along with his Archbishop. Thomas More, a devout Catholic, had been unable to go along with the new marriage and had already resigned as Chancellor leaving Thomas Cromwell, Earl of Essex, as Chief Minister.

Nor was life running smoothly in the royal household. Anne's prickly personality created many enemies in court, including Cromwell. So, although she had had a daughter, Elizabeth, when she failed to produce a son and heir she must have realised that her fate was sealed. Equally the Catholic Church in England must have worried about its standing as Henry began rounding up those who failed to recognise the Act of Supremacy following his break with Rome and the closure of the monasteries. There was a groundswell of anti-Catholic feeling in mainland Europe driven by the general population's anger at the great wealth of the church. In England, by contrast, the antagonism came from the top; Henry wanted his marriage declared null and void and the church stood in his way. Most people in England held no ill-feeling towards the church.

Henry must also have been aware that he was about to get his hands on a new source of income. To put this in context, at the time one man in 50 was in holy orders, there were some 900 religious houses, and together the church owned about a quarter of nation's wealth.[45] The monasteries, friaries, and convents with their extensive land holding must have been a tempting bonus. We should remember that the idea of 'disbanding' monasteries and nunneries and relocating the religious to larger houses thereby freeing up the revenue was not new: Cardinal Wolsey was not alone in seeing the potential when he dissolved St Frideswhite's Priory – now Oxford Cathedral – in order to help bankroll his own Christ Church, Oxford.

The first Suppression of Religious Houses Act in 1535 ironically targeted monasteries and convents which were alleged to be failing in their religious practice, as well of course of failing to swear to the Act of Supremacy. Cromwell dispatched inspectors essentially to do an inventory of both the property and the morals of the religious orders. Closure in some cases could be avoided on payment of heavy fines and where they could not be paid, property was seized, and imprisonment and execution often followed.

In the context of this book the dissolution of the monasteries was a successful money raising venture – producing in today's terms some £36 million per annum – but in itself did nothing to help Henry who, in 1536, gave up hope of Anne Boleyn ever producing a son, and was now more interested in his new mistress, Jane Seymour, one of Anne's ladies-in-waiting. Anne was arrested on trumped-up charges of treasonous adultery and incest, and executed on 19 May. The very next day Henry and Jane became engaged and were married 10 days later.

Jane quickly did her duty by Henry and produced a son, the future Edward VI, but the birth was difficult and Jane died less than a fortnight later. Henry soon recovered from his sorrow, and possibly at the instigation of Cromwell, a new potential bride, Anne of Cleves, was found. But perhaps Holbein's painting of her to tempt the King flattered to deceive because in short order, Henry wanted his marriage to Anne annulled so he could marry another, Catherine Howard, niece of the Duke of Norfolk. Anne consented, was given a generous allowance, and made 'the King's

---

45 A. G. Dickens, *The English Reformation* (Fontana Press, 1986).

sister'. Cromwell on the other hand was given the blame for the failed marriage and quickly fell out of favour with the King before being found guilty of treason, among other offences, and executed.

Unfortunately, Catherine had history as they say, or more correctly had a past she would have preferred to conceal. Under questioning by Cranmer she admitted to an affair with Francis Dereham before her marriage, and under torture, he soon identified Thomas Culpeper as the Queen's current lover. All three were executed in 1542.

That same year all the remaining monasteries in the country were dissolved, providing Henry with much needed revenue for a new assault on France in support of the Emperor Charles planned for 1543. Meanwhile, he took time to launch an attack on Scotland, which was still staunchly Catholic, for having reneged on the Treaty of Greenwich by which the then seven-month-old Mary, later Queen of Scots, would become betrothed to Prince Edward. Henry wanted Mary to be handed over to him, presumably to be prepared for her future life as Queen. In addition, the Scots had renewed their alliance with France. It was too much for Henry who sent Edward's uncle, Edward Seymour, north to put Scotland to 'the fire and the sword'.[46] It became known as the 'Rough Wooing'.

The much delayed invasion of France went ahead in 1544 but it was a lame campaign. Henry managed to capture Boulogne but refused to attack Paris, and the Emperor eventually made peace with France. In the end, with both France and England broke, Henry returned Boulogne in exchange for the equivalent of £750,000. The campaigning had cost him £650,000.[47]

In the end, Henry's campaigning in France and Scotland had cost the country dearly and it would take decades for the economy to recover; Crown land had to be sold, the currency was devalued, the very modern disease of inflation was rampant, and even the gold and silver content of the coins had been reduced to such an

46 Jenny Wormald, *Mary, Queen of Scots: Politics, Passion and a Kingdom Lost* (London: Tauris Parke, 2001).
47 David Loades, *Henry VIII – Church, Court and Conflict* (The National Archives, 2009).

extent that as the coins wore down the copper shone through – hence Henry's nickname 'Old Coppernose'. This period has been dubbed the Great Debasement 1542–1551.

Henry had been creative about minting new money, often mixing base metal with silver and gold and 'passing off' the coins as having the same value as solid silver and gold. It was a scam which people eventually rumbled, and they began hoarding the genuine articles, leading to a bullion shortage. A debased currency left everyone poorer; landowners consolidated their holdings by evicting smaller tenant farmers creating large enclosed properties:

> Where they could the owners raised rents; where men could not pay for they lost their land, and faced the option of becoming wage-earning labourers or taking to the open road as vagabonds. The centuries-old system of peasants with strips of land for which they paid by tending the lord's demesne began very gradually to disappear.[48]

The need for money, in short, was changing the very look of the English countryside.

He may have inherited much, but Henry bequeathed little to his son Edward VI (1547– 1553) who was just nine when he became King.

Some of the first coins minted after Henry's death such as the shilling still bore his name with the date 1549. This may have been done for practical reasons, as existing dies could still be used. Henry himself had continued minting coins with Henry VII's name eighteen years into his reign for the same reason, later simply adding an extra digit to show Henry VIII. Alternatively, as one suggestion has it, the coins may have come from melting down the silver of coins from Henry's reign and therefore the new coins were somehow 'Henry's'. The British Numismatist Society quotes Henry Symonds paraphrase of the translation of the inscription on some groats, REDDE CIVIQUE QVOD SVVM EST, as 'Render to Henry the things that are his'.[49]

48 Roy Strong, *The Story of Britain* (Hutchinson, 1996).
49 www.britnumsoc.org

As Edward was still a child, his uncle and sixteen executors had been appointed by Henry as his advisors, and as soon as Henry died they quickly manoeuvred among themselves for titles and possessions: Edward Seymour became Governor of the King's Person and Lord Protector of the Realm – a title Henry had not created – appointing himself 1st Duke of Somerset. Seymour and Cranmer were determined to maintain and expand the Protestant teaching in England, and although Henry was known for his break with Rome, it was during Edward's reign that Protestantism was firmly established. The mass was abolished and all services were conducted in English; Cranmer's *Book of Common Prayer* is still used today. Statues were removed and stained glass windows replaced with plain glass; colourful religious wall paintings were painted over with whitewash to reflect the new austere look.

Seymour's rise to power in 1547 seems to have been matched only by the speed of his decline. Fighting in Scotland and France proved costly; when the French attacked Boulogne English forces were clearly overstretched and he was forced to withdraw from Scotland. His opponents on the Regency Council were gathering ammunition against him, and there was unrest at home with rebellions against the imposition of the Common Prayer Book and against landlords encroaching on common land to expand their estates and, of course, raise more money. John Dudley, Earl of Warwick, became leader of the opposition against Seymour. In 1552, with no support from the young King, Seymour was accused of plotting against the council and was executed.

Dudley was made Duke of Northumberland, and where once he was regarded as an opportunist and a schemer, opinion has now shifted to credit him with returning the economy of the country to a sounder, if not yet solid, footing, after a momentary hiccough when he debased the currency again for short-term profit.

If Edward was not directly involved in the day-to-day affairs of state, he was nonetheless growing into a confirmed Protestant, which enabled Cranmer and Northumberland to pursue the policies set in train by Seymour. This meant that church property was seized and chantries – essentially trusts endowed with financial donations, lands, and rents, all of which went to priests to pray for deceased relatives – were dissolved. In short, they were a source of highly lucrative income which now went straight to the Crown. The church was left financially destitute and its vast properties distributed to loyal supporters.

But Edward was not a healthy child, and all thought of further reform had to be put on hold as the council worried about succession. The last thing they wanted was his Catholic half-sister, Mary Tudor, to be crowned; indeed, historians are of the view that this was also Edward's firmly held belief, which lead to a document called the 'Device for Succession,' in which Lady Jane Grey, Edward's first cousin once removed and Northumberland's daughter-in-law, was chosen to be Queen, excluding Mary and her sister, Elizabeth, on the grounds that they were illegitimate. On 6 July 1553, Edward died, most probably from tuberculosis, and four days later Jane was proclaimed Queen. However, such was the support for Mary I (1553–1558) that Jane was persuaded by her own father to step aside. It didn't save them, and in February 1554, Jane, her husband, and her father were all beheaded.

Mary I

Mary, a devout Roman Catholic, misread her popular support, which was simply in favour of legitimate succession, and set about trying to undo the Protestant changes that had been imposed during Henry and Edward's reigns. But it proved to be an unpopular decision. Some 300, including Cranmer, refused to convert, which was regarded as treason, and were burned at the stake earning her the sobriquet 'Bloody Mary,' while many noblemen refused to return the properties seized from the church as Mary tried to reinstate monastic orders. The last straw was her decision to marry Prince Philip of Spain, who later became King of Spain in 1556, hoping to produce an heir. If Mary had expected that the country would benefit economically from the Spanish share in New World Trade, it was not to be, and the marriage simply embroiled the country in Spain's war with France. As for Philip, he clearly regarded it as a marriage of convenience. His aide Ruy Gómez de Silva wrote: 'the marriage was concluded for no fleshly consideration, but in order to remedy the disorders of this kingdom and to preserve the Low Countries'.[50] Regardless, the marriage failed to produce any children to continue Mary's Catholic line and she was succeeded by Elizabeth I (1558–1603), who had survived a testing apprenticeship, enduring two accusations of treason and a period locked up in the Tower of London.

Given her nine day 'reign' there was no time for Lady Jane Grey to issue any coins, although there have been mischievous claims of some discoveries. Mary, by contrast, immediately set to work, and we have detailed accounts of the coinage she demanded and indeed her view on what should be done to those who let her down.

Just six weeks into her reign she issued a proclamation stating her intention to produce 'coynes as well as of gold as of silver of the perfect fineness',[51] and where the moneyers or engravers fell short or tried to be fraudulent through clipping or creating false dies then they should be tortured 'if thought to be convenient'.[52] Following her marriage to Philip the following list of coins and their respective values was released:

of fine gold:

the sovereign to be valued of 30s
the royal to be valued at 15s
the angel to be valued at 10s
the half angel to be valued at 5s

---

50 Calendar of State Papers, Spanish Volume XIII.
51 www.britnumsoc.org
52 www.britnumsoc.org

of fine silver:

the shilling to be valued at 12d
the half shilling to be valued at 6d
the groat to be valued at 4d[53]

In fact the angel and the half angel were the only gold coins to have been found, which points to a shortage of bullion.[54]

But throughout this period there was always the troublesome issue of Scotland for the monarchs of England.

THE SCOTTISH KINGS AND A QUEEN

The arrival of Mary, Queen of Scots, prompts the question: how had Scotland been managing its currency if for so many years it had been at war with its closest neighbour and seemingly perennial rival if not enemy? Even in the 21st century the Scots could not have been clearer when they returned 56 Scottish National Party MPs out of 59 available seats to Westminster Parliament in the 2015 General Election that they wanted to do things differently. In the Middle Ages they preferred to count France as an ally rather than reach any sort of peaceful co-existence with England.

In the mid-13th century there were 16 mints operating in Scotland, and designs and names would, over time, reflect continental influence from Germany and France: the 'dollar' (thaler) and the 'testoun' (from the French *tête*–head). Remember, the Scots resented the English still holding territory in southern Scotland when Robert II was King, and it wasn't until 1384 that the land was retaken.

The reign of Robert III (1390–1406) was a sad time. He was also old – 53 – by contemporary standards when he succeeded his brother, and he was dominated by his younger brother, the Duke of Albany. Coins were issued in his name but his whole kingdom was condemned by one chronicler as 'a den of thieves'[55] and Robert

Robert III

53 www.britnumsoc.org
54 www.britnumsoc.org
55 www.stewartsociety.org

himself said they should write on his tombstone: 'Here lies the worst of kings and the most wretched of men.'[56]

Officially Robert was succeeded by his young son, James I (1406–1437), but he had been captured by English pirates en route to France, where ironically he was being sent for his own safety from the squabbling Scottish nobles, and handed over to Henry IV. His uncle, the Duke of Albany, was appointed Governor of Scotland while his nephew was a minor and absent, but he was in no rush to pay a ransom for James's release, and the boy-king remained a captive, albeit one who was well cared for and educated, for the next 18 years. Eventually, in 1423 £40,000 was paid to win his freedom. James immediately set about trying to restore some order to the unruly Scottish earls, executing opponents and seizing their lands; he must have been thinking about all this while he languished in his gilded captivity. Inevitably his reprisals caused ill-feeling and in 1437 conspirators, led by his own uncle, Walter, Earl of Atholl, murdered him.

His son, James II (1437–1460), was six when he succeeded his father, which once again triggered rivalry for control of the kingdom among the nobility, with the Douglas family dominating the court during the King's infancy. But it was a dangerous time to be a Douglas: the 6th Earl and his brother were murdered in 1440 at the so-called 'Black Dinner' at Edinburgh Castle when James was still only ten. Then in 1452, James himself stabbed the 8th Earl to death during a drunken argument at Stirling Castle, only for the 9th Earl to later be accused of treason. But luck wasn't on James's side either, as one of his own cannons exploded when he was standing next to, it killing him instantly when he was aged just 29, leaving his nine-year-old son, James III (1460–1488), to succeed him.

When he began to rule for himself in 1469 James faced the seemingly endless rivalry with the Scottish nobility and problems with his English neighbour, Edward IV. James was not cut from the typical fierce fighting stock of many kings of the time, preferring instead the company of scholars and artists; the coinage he had struck was notable in both Scotland and England in being the first

56 Geoff Holder, *Bloody British History: Britain* (The History Press).

to bear at least a passing resemblance to the monarch of the day.

However, James had problems closer to home; he accused his own brothers of treason, most notably the Duke of Albany who, having failed twice to overthrow the King, eventually escaped to France. Finally, in 1488, James was defeated at the Battle of Sauchiebaum by the Scottish nobles; he fell from his horse when he tried to escape and, as he lay injured in a bed, was stabbed to death.

James III

We are now only part-way through the long run of five King James's of Scotland who ruled from 1406–1542, making it easy for the mints as the coins all bore the same IACOBUS and generally without a regnal numeral. But there was an insistence on quality as made clear in Acts of Parliament. One, in 1484 during the reign of James IV (1488–1513) when ordering the striking of a gold coin, stated: '...and a penny of silvir to be equale in finance to the auld Inglis groit...'[57] It wouldn't do to be inferior to the English groat.

James IV must have seemed like a breath of fresh air after so much blood-letting in Scotland; he was highly-educated, spoke six languages including Latin, French, and German, and he finally managed to bring order to his nation, conquering the last of the rebellious nobles. He even managed to find some accord with England despite, as we have seen, his initial support for Perkin Warbeck's claim to the English throne in 1502. When his mistress, Margaret Drummond, died he agreed to marry Henry VII's daughter, Princess Margaret Tudor, paving the way to what would eventually lead to unification under one ruler. Before that could be achieved though, when Henry VIII invaded France in 1513, James felt he had no choice but to support Scotland's long-time allies and lead his own army south into England. The outcome as we know was a crushing defeat for the Scots at the Battle of Flodden, where James was killed.

The Scots may have been accustomed to minors on the throne, but James V (1513–1542) was only a year old when he succeeded

THE TUDOR DYNASTY

his father leaving his mother, Margaret Tudor, briefly as Regent. That was never going to last and she was replaced by James's uncle, the Duke of Albany. Life for the King became a tangle when his mother remarried then promptly divorced her second husband, Archibald Douglas, 6th Earl of Angus, who effectively kidnapped James, holding him a virtual prisoner for more than two years before James managed to escape.

Now his own man, James set about taking revenge, driving his erstwhile kidnapper out of Scotland and settling a few other scores. John Knox, the Scottish clergyman and writer, called him, '... a good poor man's king; of others he was termed a murderer of nobility, one that had decreed their whole destruction...'[58]

He married twice: the first time to Princess Madeleine of France who died within weeks of her arrival in Scotland, and then to the French widow, Mary of Guise. Together they had two sons, who both died in infancy, and a daughter, the future Mary, Queen of Scots.

James was a devout Catholic and turned down his uncle Henry VIII's urging to follow his lead and break with Rome. When James failed to meet Henry at York in 1541, Henry invaded Scotland. James mobilised an army and marched south to meet him but his army was defeated at the Battle of Solway Moss in 1542. Although James was not there, he collapsed on hearing the news and retired to his bed at Falkland Palace in Fife. He died just six days after Mary was born.

Two influences can be found in James V coinage: one is the power of the Douglas family when, for a time, Sir Archibald Douglas was Lord High Treasurer and changed the moneyer employed in the striking of gold and silver in return for a minimum annual payment of £3,000 Scots per annum. The second was in the design of the crown which resembled the French *écu*, clearly underlining where Scotland's loyalties lay.[59]

About this time coins were produced almost exclusively in Edinburgh, although the Stirling mint produced for the first time during James V's reign one issue of the bawbee – a Scottish halfpenny worth six Scots pence.

58 John Knox, *The History of the Reformation of Religion in Scotland*.
59 www.britnumsoc.org

Bawbee, James V

As an infant just days old, Mary, Queen of Scots (1542–1567) was dependent on regents to govern for her, split between the pro-France and pro-England lobbies. Her French mother, Mary of Guise, naturally decided that the best place for her to spend her childhood was in France in the royal court. Having spurned the proposed betrothal to Henry VIII's son, the future Edward VI, and recovered from the subsequent 'Rough Wooing' in 1558, she married the Dauphin of France, who on becoming King Francis II the following year made Mary briefly Queen Consort of France; briefly because Francis died 17 months later. Mary was still only 17 and had a difficult decision to make: stay in France or take her chances in Scotland, where after all she was Queen in her own right, notwithstanding the fact that it was now a Protestant country.

She decided that she would prefer to return to Scotland rather than live under the shadow of her mother-in-law, Catherine de Medicis. She immediately adopted a conciliatory approach and recognised the Reformed (Presbyterian) Church while continuing to be a practising Catholic herself. But she ended up not pleasing anyone, and even true love seemed to elude her. Having been rejected by Don Carlos, son of King Philip II of Spain, she married her first cousin, Henry Stewart, Lord Darnley in 1565. This marriage soon soured and she came to rely on her secretary, David Rizzio, for advice and solace. Darnley probably encouraged a Protestant-inspired whispering campaign against Rizzio, suggesting he was too friendly with the Queen and possibly a papal spy, and had him murdered in front of Mary's eyes in Holyrood Palace. She was six months pregnant at the time with the future James VI of Scotland and James I of England. 31. Mary & Darnley

In 1567, a mysterious fire was started in Darnley's home and he was found murdered in the garden with the finger of suspicion pointing at James Hepburn, 4th Earl of Bothwell, who, having been acquitted of all charges, duly married Mary in April that year. But she had burned too many bridges; people could not understand why she would marry a man suspected of murdering her husband, and having been forced to abdicate in favour of her son, she fled south to seek protection from her cousin, Elizabeth, by now Queen of England. As we shall see, it would prove to be another mistake. Bothwell meanwhile escaped to Denmark only to be captured and held in captivity there for the rest of his life.

The coins tell their own story. Once again, during Mary's reign in Scotland, the French influence in the coinage struck at the time is clear; indeed the gold crowns are obviously based on the French *écu au soleil*, and although the gold quality was inferior, the Scottish and French crowns were given the same value.

When Mary and Darnley married the occasion was marked with the striking of a ryal silver coin worth 30 Scots shillings and depicting Mary facing Darnley with the legend: 'Mary and Henry, Queen and King of the Scots'. The first version of these coins had their names reversed but these were quickly recalled.

James VI (1567–1625) was 13 months old when he ascended the throne – he had already seen his mother for the last time – and inevitably the Scottish nobles sought to influence him their way. He nevertheless grew up managing to bring some degree of reconciliation between the warring factions; opinions vary on just how shrewd a King he was – Henry IV of France called him 'the wisest fool in Christendom'. All the same he would succeed in at least one ambition: becoming King of England and Scotland.

Mary and Darnley

7 THE ELIZABETHAN ERA

If Mary had been expecting a warm reception from her cousin Elizabeth I (1558–1603), she was to be quickly disabused. It was too dangerous to have Mary, the focus of Catholic supporters, wandering freely in the kingdom, particularly as Elizabeth had claimed the English throne for herself, so Mary was held in comfortable captivity for 19 years. During this time inquiries were conducted to see if Mary herself had been complicit in Darnley's murder – the so-called Casket Letters allegedly written by Mary were produced in evidence. In the end the plotting against Elizabeth, most notably the Babington Plot,[60] became too much and Mary was executed at Fotheringhay Castle in 1587.

Elizabeth was the last of the Tudor dynasty and wasted no time in ensuring her reign was secure from religious strife by extracting a working compromise between the Protestant and Roman Catholic faiths in the 39 Articles of 1563.

The reputation of the monarchy was also at stake. Murder, plots, and executions had dominated the country for too long and one other thing had fallen into disrepute – the currency. It was so debased that it could not be trusted at home, or worse, abroad.

Elizabeth appointed Sir Thomas Gresham as her chief financial adviser, who set about restoring confidence in the coinage by withdrawing the debased currency between 1560 and 1561, melting it down and re-issuing fine quality Elizabethan coins of silver and gold, making a tidy profit of £50,000 for the Crown in the process. Gresham's Law – bad money drives out good – is named after him. He also funded an exchange in London in 1569 which later became the Royal Exchange following a visit by the Queen.

---

60 Apart from seeking to restore Mary to the throne of England, the plot included encouraging an invasion by Philip II of Spain and returning the country to Roman Catholicism.

A rare silver medal was struck to mark the occasion, showing Elizabeth in all her glory on the obverse. Elizabeth is also recorded as visiting the Royal Mint in the Tower of London in 1561, which underlines how much importance she gave to the strengthening of English coinage.

Among the many new coins which were struck during her reign the ryal, worth 15 shillings, which appeared between 1584 and 1589, tells us something about Elizabeth's delicately judged diplomatic policies. She tried to juggle her relationship with Catholic Spain and its desire to impose Catholicism on what was known as the Spanish Netherlands, consisting of present-day Holland

Elizabeth I

and Belgium. Initially, Elizabeth lent her discreet financial support to English volunteers fighting Spain, but when Philip II dispatched his military commander, Alexander Farnese, to retake control of the region, Elizabeth responded by sending a force under Robert Dudley, Earl of Leicester, on an expensive and largely fruitless counter-offensive paid for in ryals. Greater success at sea was to follow.

In July 1588, the mighty Spanish Armada set sail essentially with two missions: to punish the English for executing Mary, Queen of Scots, and by supplying forces through controlling the English Channel. The fatal flaw in the Spanish plan, of course, was that the impregnable crescent formation of the Spanish fleet had to break up in order to put into port to take on men and supplies in France before the invasion of England, which left the fleet vulnerable to attack from Sir Francis Drake's fire ships.

Less often discussed in history classes is the overwhelming defeat by Spain of the 'English Armada' the following year led by

Sir Francis, with a heavy loss of life and some 40 ships. The threat from Spanish attack with the Anglo-Spanish War (1585–1604) was a constant theme throughout the latter part of Elizabeth's reign, and a costly one, which is a nice irony as Elizabeth endorsed the striking of a coin called the tester or testoon – a 2s silver coin with a portcullis emblem – that was minted to the equivalent weight in silver of the Spanish *real*. This coin was produced predominantly for merchants trading in the East Indies because the Indians were used to Spanish coins, which reminds us about England's far-reaching ambitions set in train by John Cabot during Henry VII's reign. On 31 December 1600 Elizabeth granted a charter to a 'Company of Merchants trading into the East Indies'; in time it developed into the all-powerful East India Company which, within 14 years, owned 24 ships.

The Empire itself was beginning to grow as England entered what is known as the Golden Age, and somehow it is appropriate that there should have been the same 'expansive' coinage to match the coming of this Golden Age. The symbol of Britannia, last seen on the coins of Roman Emperors, would not appear until the reign of Charles II, but she was featuring in contemporary drama and literature as English ships came to dominate the waves around our islands and far beyond.

At the very top of the tree so to speak there was the fine sovereign, also known as the double noble. There was the lesser crown sovereign, the ryal we have mentioned, and the Angel worth 10s. There were smaller denominations – such as the half angel and quarter angel – as well as the popular testoon worth 12d, which was the dominant coin in circulation. Among the other denominations around at the time were the sixpence, half groat and, of course, the penny – the most basic coin in daily use by the working people which had been minted almost without break since AD 790. A penny might have bought you some bread or a chicken, a half penny a tankard of ale, while 2d would have bought you a room in an inn for a few days.

The reality for most people was that they only required 'small change,' but as the value of coins at the time was based on the precious metal content it became difficult to produce small enough coins with sufficient value. As a result merchants themselves produced tokens make of lead, tin, or even leather, which they readily accepted in exchange for goods. 33. Token, Elizabeth I Indeed, tokens had been used in Western Europe since Roman times; however, they did nothing for the Exchequer as no taxes were paid on them.

But this was a time of prosperity and flowering of literature and adventure for England – there was Shakespeare, Marlowe, Drake, and Columbus – and the nation was also faring better than its Continental rivals in Italy where the Italian Renaissance was coming to an end. France throughout much of the 16th century was mired in the Wars of Religion (1562–1598) between the Catholic League and the Protestant Huguenots, only ending with the Edict of Nantes, which granted the Huguenots the right to practise their religion without fear of persecution. Spain on the other hand, despite the setback for the Spanish Armada, inflicted defeats on the English and lent its support to the long running Irish Catholic rebellion, placing a drain on the Treasury. The Nine Year War with the Irish only ended a few days after Elizabeth's death and a peace treaty with Spain was only signed a year later – the Treaty of London 1604.

Elizabeth and her ministers had set about turning England's financial fortunes round from one of near bankruptcy. For a time the Crown enjoyed a surplus of £300,000, although that had turned into a debt of £350,000 by the time of Elizabeth's death because of the cost of the Anglo-Spanish War and the campaigns in the Netherlands.[61]

Elizabeth I

Nevertheless, taxes were lower than other European countries and the economy was expanding.

Although Europe may have still been slow in the inventiveness of some of its sciences and academic prowess compared with the Middle, Near, and Far East that was about to change; in the

61 Melissa D. Aaron, *Global Economics* (University of Delaware Press, 2006)

meantime, per head of population, from an economic standpoint, it was already ahead:

Western European GDP per capita was higher than that of both China and India by 1500; by 1600, it was 50% higher than China's. From there, the gap kept growing. Between 1350 and 1950 – six hundred years – GDP per capita remained roughly constant on China and India (hovering around $600 for China and $550 for India). In the same period, Western European GDP per capita went from $662 to $4,594, a 594 percent increase.[62]

As Elizabeth's health declined and many of her loyal ministers began to die, the inevitable jockeying for position in court increased with Sir Robert Cecil, who had assumed the position of senior political adviser in 1598 on the death of his father, the loyal, and long-serving Lord Burghley, promoting the cause of James VI of Scotland.

62 Fareed Zakaria, *The Post-American World* (Penguin, 2009).

8 THE STUART DYNASTY

1603–1714

James ascended the Scottish throne on 24 July 1567 when his
mother, Mary, Queen of Scots, was forced to abdicate, and her
illegitimate half-brother, James Stewart, Earl of Moray, was
appointed as the first of four regents. Although he was baptised
'Charles James' in a Catholic ceremony in Stirling Castle, James
was brought up as a Protestant in the Church of Scotland; at his
coronation the sermon was delivered by John Knox, the founder
of the Presbyterian denomination in Scotland.

The early years of James's reign in Scotland were dominated by
in-fighting and inevitable favouritism – he was said to be overly
fond of Esmé Stewart (later Duke of Lennox), first cousin of Lord
Darnley, James's father, and others were to follow prompting the
epigram *Rex fuit Elizabeth, nunc est regina Jacobus* ('Elizabeth
was King, now James is Queen'). At one point James himself was
'kidnapped,' held in Ruthven Castle, and was only released when
Lennox was forced out of Scotland.

In due course James assumed some control of the country,
but it was in a precarious financial state and the intervention of
an eight man commission, the Octavians, essentially a tax-raising
body, only led to unrest on the streets of Edinburgh. Despite his
disrupted childhood and the pressure of his first tutor, George
Buchanan, who beat him regularly, to get him to hate his Catholic
mother, James grew up to be a remarkably level-headed and
intellectual King, despite the epithet handed down by Henry VI
of France.

Fool or not, he was wise enough to sign the Treaty of Berwick
in 1586 uniting England and Scotland; indeed, such was his
ambition to become King of England that when Elizabeth signed
his mother's death warrant he could only muster mild objection
– 'a preposterous and strange procedure' – paving the way to his

becoming King of England on Elizabeth's death. The following year he further endeared himself to the Protestant cause by marrying Anne of Denmark by whom he had eight children, including the future King Charles I.

On 24 March 1603 James was proclaimed King James I of England (1603–1625), Scotland, France,[63] and Ireland in succession to his cousin, and ushered in the House of Stuart in an extraordinarily smooth transition of power. Despite some opposition, James preferred to be known as King of Great Britain, France, and Ireland, and as a result, in 1604 the second major coinage of his reign bore a new coat of arms with the arms of France and England, quarterly, in the 1st and 4th quarters; those of Scotland in the 2nd; and those of Ireland in the 3rd.[64]

There were three main periods of coinage during his reign: the first on his accession, the second between 1604 and 1619, importantly bearing the inscription of King of Great Britain as the obverse legend, and the third period, 1619–1625, when most of the coins were minted, reflecting perhaps his demand for more cash. Indeed, on 19 May 1613 James issued a proclamation banning the tokens which had been circulating since Elizabeth's reign, and granted Lord Harrington a patent to produce an official copper farthing token from which both the King and Harrington hoped to profit. The coins, with a crown and crossed sceptres on the obverse and crowned harp on the reverse, were so small and lightweight that there were protests and the weight had to be increased. In addition they were easily counterfeited.

James's ambition to unite England and Scotland is well illustrated in a hoard of 59 gold coins found during building work at a site in Chipping

James I

63 James, like other English monarchs between 1340–1800, styled himself King of France, although he did not rule the country.

64 www.predecimal.com

Norton, Oxfordshire, in 2009. They were worth 20s and were dubbed the 'unites' as they are engraved with the words FACIAM EOS IN GENTEM UNAM ('I will make one nation').

Meanwhile, in Ireland the first coins James issued in 1603 and again in 1604 to improve the quality of the coinage were shillings and sixpences struck in silver with a prominent harp on the reverse.

James was probably delighted to be able to leave Scotland behind after all the murder and intrigue which dominated his boyhood days – he only returned there once (1617) after becoming King of England, happy to rule 'by the stroke of a pen'. However, while the transition of power may have been smooth, he had his opponents in the south, not least among the Catholics who, led by Robert Catesby and including the better-known Guy Fawkes, tried to blow up the King and his ministers in the infamous Gunpowder Plot at the State Opening of Parliament on 5 November 1605. The Protestants also bridled somewhat when the King failed to introduce some of the more Puritanical teachings of the Scottish kirk, notwithstanding the publication in 1611 of the Authorised King James Bible, which to this day is regarded as a masterpiece of English literature and the standard text.

James believed in the divine right of kings to rule, as set out in his *True Law of Free Monarchies*, and that would bring him into conflict with his Parliament when he demanded more money to pursue his ambitions, as the Royal Mint was not always in his grasp. Parliament, he argued, was merely a tool of kingship. There were kings he wrote,

> before any estates or ranks of men, before any parliaments were holden, or laws made, and by them was the land distributed, which at first was wholly theirs. And so it follows of necessity that kings were the authors and makers of the laws, and not the laws of the kings.[65]

His problems began almost as soon as he was crowned as he wanted to unite the kingdoms of England and Scotland and

65 David Harris Willson, *King James VI and I* (Jonathan Cape, 1965).

suspended Parliament when it failed to back his plans for the union. Parliament also disliked the way he lavished gifts and titles on his favourites including George Villiers, whom he ennobled as the Duke of Buckingham and was later to become a disastrous influence in the country's foreign affairs.

This was followed in 1610 by the clash with Robert Cecil and his ideas to reform the royal finances, which by then were in disarray. Under the terms of the 'Great Contract' James would have received an annual sum if he abandoned the traditional feudal rights of the King of England. The numbers were huge: the royal debt was £300,000 and James said he needed £200,000 a year to live as befitted a king.

The Commons resisted Cecil's urgings as MPs demanded more concessions from the monarchy. James meanwhile was annoyed by their endless debating, not to mention the fact that the whole country now knew about his weak financial position. In the end the Great Contract foundered when James lost patience with the protracted negotiations and once again dismissed Parliament on 31 December 1610. The Contract may not have actually solved the problem, but James would spend the rest of his reign struggling to balance the books.

James was frustrated:

The House of Commons is a body without a head. The members give their opinion in a disorderly manner; at their meetings nothing is heard but cries, shouts and confusion. I am surprised that my ancestors should ever have permitted such an institution to come into existence.[66]

His problems continued when he dismissed the so-called 'Addled Parliament' after just eight weeks in 1614 when it became clear that the MPs wanted to challenge his insistence on the right to raise money without the consent of Parliament. The 1621 Parliament was equally short-lived, with James vowing never to have anything further to do with the Commons. Three years later

---

66 Winston Churchill, *A History of the English Speaking Peoples Volume II: The New World.*

he had to backtrack when once more England found itself at war with Spain, and Parliament was recalled to raise funds, which this time it agreed to do, although not as much as James wanted.

The Spanish War was an ill-conceived venture from the start, which James almost stumbled into, trying and failing to balance Catholic and Protestant causes. He married off his daughter, Princess Elizabeth, to Frederick, the Elector Palatine, head of the Calvanist princes of Germany, and wanted his son and heir, Prince Henry, to marry the Infanta, Maria Anna of Spain, daughter of Philip III. This potential union of the great Catholic and Protestant royal families of Europe was strongly resisted by Parliament. James even tried to curry favour with Spain by executing Sir Walter Raleigh for attacking Spanish vessels. The long drawn-out 'courtship' orchestrated by Buckingham ended with the premature death of Prince Henry aged just 18, possibly from typhoid.

The religious tension in Europe was toxic. The Thirty Years War (1618–1648), essentially a fight between Catholics and Protestants struggling for control in a disintegrating Holy Roman Empire, was spiralling out of control. James thought he could bring about peace by marrying Charles to a Catholic, the Habsburg Princess Maria Anna of Spain. But this proposal simply infuriated Parliament, while both James and Charles thought Parliament was impertinent to interfere in these matters.

It was James's seemingly endless conflict with Parliament and his insistence that he was always right which many regard as the root cause of the civil war which was to follow.

Charles I

Charles I (1625–1649) seemed to have learned nothing from his father's travails with Parliament and clearly was determined to carry on in much the same vein once he came of age, proclaiming the divine right of monarchs to rule as they wished. Indeed, within months of his accession he married another Catholic, the 15-year-old princess, Henrietta Maria, the youngest daughter of Henry IV of France.

It was not a good start as far as his ministers and possibly people were concerned. Henrietta Maria was never crowned Queen, and as the hostile climate increased leading to civil war, she would eventually have to flee for her own safety to France.

Even before his father's death, Charles had already become close to Buckingham, further inflaming the English Parliament over the promotion of favourites. It was Buckingham and Charles who had encouraged James to declare war on Spain following Charles's failure to woo the Spanish Infanta.

In the first part of Charles's reign the coins produced were fairly typical of a new monarch. There was a new gold denomination – the triple unite; there were silver coins depicting the king on horseback, apparently confident of his power and supremacy; shillings, pennies and groats, and all produced by the mint in the Tower of London, or in a new mint which opened in Aberystwyth to take advantage of the output from the Welsh silver mines. But it was during the civil war period (1642–1648) that the inventiveness of the moneyers tells the most interesting tales as mints sprang up in unexpected places, producing what might be called an alternative currency.

We should pause a moment to understand the 'politics' of the land at the time. Parliament was only summoned by the monarch to do his bidding, which effectively meant raising the taxes he needed. He didn't expect any dissent and was able to dissolve Parliament whenever he chose.

But monarchs could not ignore Parliament, precisely because it had the revenue-generating hold over them. Charles's marriage to Henrietta Maria had not gone down well and Parliament made its displeasure felt by making it difficult for him to collect taxes due to him without regular negotiations.

He might have won some favour had an expedition to relieve the Siege of La Rochelle in 1627, where the French Huguenots were pitted against the Catholic forces of Louis XIII, proved more successful. It was a disaster and Parliament blamed the leadership of Charles's favourite, Buckingham, who was impeached.

Charles responded by dissolving Parliament, but that meant he could not raise any more money, a problem he solved simply by appointing a new one in 1628; among its members was one Oliver Cromwell. In effect, this was Charles taking matters into his own hands – 'the Personal Rule' – which lasted for eleven years. During this time he managed to antagonise the Scots by trying to impose a form of High Anglicanism – Catholicism by the backdoor – on the Church of Scotland. It resulted in a series of battles with the 'Covenanters,' who rose up in the Bishops' Wars of 1639 and 1640, which left the Scots occupying large tracts of northern England.

Charles was out of money and had no choice in April 1640 but to recall Parliament, which took the opportunity of criticising him and refused to discuss any of his demands before even considering a new tax. For its impudence, the King promptly dissolved Parliament once again; hence the 'Short Parliament'.

But his position was untenable, and faced with increased threats from the Scots, who were demanding payment from the Crown to stop any further encroachment over the border, Charles had no choice but to recall Parliament in November – the 'Long Parliament'. Very quickly laws were passed preventing the King from raising taxes without permission and insisting on Parliament convening at least once every three years.

In fact, England was not a regularly taxed country, and it was hard to raise funds for military adventures at home or overseas. There was no standing army and the King had to rely on volunteers and mercenaries, all of whom demanded payment. To sidestep Parliament Charles raised money by reviving old taxes such as 'ship money'. The original idea was to use this tax, imposed only on coastal districts, in times of war, but Charles decided that the country needed to protect its coastal waters at all times. Between 1634 and 1638 the levy raised between £150,000 and £200,000 every year and payment was demanded from all, including inland areas.[67]

The reality in 1640 was that Charles was essentially bankrupt. He had antagonised land owners by extending boundaries of the royal forests to previous limits and demanding rent, he had exasperated merchants in the City of London simply by seizing £130,000 held in trust in the Tower of London, and he had even seized the stocks of pepper held by the East India Company and sold them off at knock-down prices.[68]

The differences between the monarch and Parliament were soon irreconcilable and the country was slipping inevitably towards civil war, the Royalists (Cavaliers) against the Parliamentarians (Roundheads). At least, the supporters of Parliament and those of Charles were heading for war; most of the rural community were largely indifferent at the outset and just wanted to get on with their lives.

The first engagement was at the Battle of Powick Bridge, near Worcester, in 1642, resulting in victory for the Royalists led by Prince Rupert of Germany, one of Charles's nephews and a formidable cavalry commander.

The battle fortunes swung both ways, but Charles was forced to try to consolidate his position outside of London, centring on Oxford. While the Parliamentarians continued to issue coins in Charles's name from the Tower mint, which was now in their hands along with all the financial resources of London, Charles himself had to open mints in cities under his authority including Oxford, Exeter, Worcester, and Shrewsbury. Coins of the day, such as the gold triple unite, bore the declaration RELIG PROT ANG LIBER PAR – 'The religion of the Protestants the laws of England and the liberty of Parliament,' which spoke volumes about the tensions in the country.

The first civil war ended with Charles being held by the Scots in 1646, but he continued to resist demands for a constitutional

---

67 Charles Carlton, Charles I: The Personal Monarch (Routledge, 1995).
68 William Scott, The Constitution and Finance of English, Scottish, and Irish Joint-Stock Companies to 1720 (Cambridge University Press, 2010).

monarchy and managed to escape his captivity briefly, only for the second civil war to flare up in 1648.

As the country inevitably divided between pro- and anti-monarchy camps, whole towns fell under siege during the fighting as they resisted the opposing forces. For our story the effect was remarkable as people demonstrated their resilience, or simply how business must go on as usual. Three Royalist towns – Carlisle, Newark, and Scarborough – fashioned their own 'coinage'.

The British Museum records the story of a 17 year old in Carlisle, Leslie Tullie, who reported in his journal that 'an order was published to every citizen to bring in their plate [silverware] to be coyned, which they did cheerfully'. The citizens on that occasion managed to produce the equiv-alent of £280 of coin through their donations of spoons and silverware. Some of these coins are ex-tremely rare today, not least because they were only in circulation for such a short time. A silver coin found in Carlisle, which was un-der siege by the Scots for a month, was sold in 2012 for £22,000.

Siege money Charles I, Charles II

As the sieges contin-ued around the country – Scarborough was un-der siege for a year – the coins produced would have been used to maintain some sense of business normality and also to pay off mercenaries who would have demanded reward for their efforts, or even those in the official armies who were known to change sides if they were not paid.[69] Although the value in weight of these various coins was accurate, the shape and designs tell their own story of the stresses and strains faced by those under siege, such as the nine pence coin found in Newark. Other coins seem to have been hacked from plates and given a stamp to indicate value and were different shapes and sizes. It was a case of needs must, and it is apparent that the citizens of the towns were ready to help even if it meant giving up their plates and spoons. Pontefract Castle in Yorkshire had faced numerous sieges, and in 1648 the Royalists fashioned diamond or lozenge shaped shillings out of gold and silver plates stamped with the letters CR for Charles and OBS for the Latin *obsessum*, meaning 'besieged', or marked DUM SPIRO SPERO ('While I Live I Hope').

Ultimately, of course, the Royalist forces were defeated; Charles was tried for high treason as a 'tyrant, traitor, murderer and public enemy'. It was too much for Sir Thomas Fairfax, who had commanded the New Model Army against the Royalists, and he stood down, leaving the way clear for Cromwell, 'Old Ironsides', his second-in-command, to take control and oversee the trial which led to the execution of Charles at Whitehall in 1649; the death warrant was co-signed by Cromwell. The monarchy was abolished and replaced with the Commonwealth.

---

69 In 1648 Parliamentary troops changed sides when they were not paid.

9 THE COMMONWEALTH AND PROTECTORATE

With no monarch or monarchy, the so-called Rump Parliament (its members severely depleted) to some extent had free rein to pass whatever laws it chose. It abolished the Privy Council and the House of Lords leaving it without any checks and balances. It passed a Bill on 19 May 1649 declaring the people of England to be under the authority of a 'Commonwealth and Free State', in short, a republic. However, it did not have a particularly cosy relationship with the army upon which it depended. Not all members wanted to be entirely rid of the monarchy, they just wanted the King's wings to be clipped; on the other hand, while many in the country regarded the Rump Parliament to be illegal, it was all that stood between them and a military takeover.

Cromwell pattern

The official mints were immediately set to work issuing coinage to reflect the new republican order, in the same way that earlier kings had quickly minted coins the moment they ascended the throne they might have usurped in order to establish, as much as anything else, their legitimacy. The typical coin designs of the time depicted the shields of England and Ireland, the date and the inscription 'God with Us' and on the obverse the legend 'Commonwealth of England' with a single shield.[70] By contrast, where there

70 www.cromwellcoins.com

had been Royalist resistance, such as during the siege of Pontefract in 1648, illegal coins were struck following Charles's execution with the inscription, 'For the son [Charles II] after the father's death'. The Royalists had not given up, despite the defeat by Cromwell's superior New Model Army of the future Charles II at the Battle of Worcester in 1651, which forced him into exile in mainland Europe and marked the end of the English Civil War.

However, it wasn't all going Cromwell's way; fighting continued in Ireland where his army's brutal treatment of the inhabitants is still a source of historical ill-feeling to this day, and in Scotland where the future Charles II had returned and been declared the rightful King. In his *A History of the English-Speaking Peoples*, Winston Churchill, commenting on troubled Anglo-Irish relations, wrote:

> ...upon all of these Cromwell's record was a lasting bane. By an uncompleted process of terror, by an iniquitous land settlement, by the virtual proscription of the Catholic religion, by the bloody deeds already described, he cut new gulfs between the nations and the creeds. 'Hell or Connaught' were the terms he thrust upon the native inhabitants, and they for their part, across three hundred years, have used as their keenest expression of hatred 'The Curse of Cromwell on you'...Upon all of us there still lies 'the curse of Cromwell'.[71]

In 1653, having had enough of the Rump Parliament's procrastinations aimed at securing its authority and position, Cromwell led his soldiers into the Commons' chamber and famously declared: 'You have sat too long for any good you have been doing lately...In the name of God, go!'

In its place, in July the following year, Cromwell established an assembly mockingly dubbed the 'Barebones Parliament' after one of its members, a radical Baptist leather goods salesman called Praise God Barbon, and in reference to the depleted (144) membership of the Assembly, most of whom were appointed by the army.

---

71 Churchill, *A History of the English-Speaking Peoples.*

By the end of the year, an army general, John Lambert, decided the country would be better off without the rather ineffectual Parliament. On 12 December, together with a group of supporters, they voted to dissolve Parliament and replace it with the Instrument of Government, appointing a Council of State and single person at its head, and that person was Cromwell, who became Lord Protector of the united 'Commonwealth of England, Scotland and Ireland' on 16 December 1653. The title of Protector was last held by Edward Seymour, Duke of Somerset, during Edward VI's minority.

THE PROTECTORATE (1653–1658)

If Cromwell was not a king he certainly behaved like one, receiving foreign ambassadors into his presence, and there was, of course, just one way to mark his appointment and underline his own legitimacy, and that was to have coins minted with his bust replacing the shields of the Commonwealth. Depicted like some sort of latter day Roman emperor complete with laurel leaves, Cromwell, the middle-class soldier who for most of his life had lived in comparative obscurity, was now the unchallenged leader of his country and soon developed ambitions to conquer further afield. There is a suggestion that the first coins minted in 1656, although most were struck in 1658, were not intended for circulation; furthermore, for coins to be legal tender required a proclamation by Parliament, but no doubt Cromwell disregarded this nicety.

Just like the King he had had executed, Cromwell quickly tired of his own first Parliament which suddenly began to have second thoughts about all the power they had bestowed upon him. His first solution was to use his soldiers to bar any member who refused to agree to his terms and finally, as the debating continued, he dissolved the Parliament in January 1655, it having failed to enact a single law.

Like so many monarchs before him, Cromwell the Protector knew that he needed funds to pay for his expensive army – his power base – not to mention his ambitions overseas. All this cost money, but he was, after all, master of all he surveyed as amply described on the 1658 half crown whose inscription reads: OLIVAR D G RP ANG SCO ET HIB &c PRO ('Oliver by the Grace of God of the Republic of England, Scotland, Ireland etc Protector').

As a first step he appointed major generals and militias to run the districts of England and Wales, ostensibly to ensure law and order, and morality, but more importantly to gather in taxes directly to his Treasury. Although there was dissent there seemed to be no appetite for real rebellion. The Penruddick Rising in 1655 found little support and was easily quashed when the rebels withdrew to South Molton in the West Country; whether the ardent Royalists wanted a return to monarchy or not, no-one was prepared to fight for it.

Cromwell, however, was all too ready for a fight, and again like monarchs in the past, thought nothing of embarking on foreign adventures, which forced him, reluctantly, to recall his second Parliament and demand more money.

His navy had already successfully engaged and defeated the Dutch in the first Anglo-Dutch War (1652–1654) and now he dispatched an expedition all the way to the West Indies to seize power in Hispaniola, but it was a failure principally because it was ill-equipped. It had more luck in Jamaica, easily overwhelming the handful of Spanish inhabitants. The island remained in British hands until 1962.

His fleet also attacked the French, defeated the Spanish at Cadiz, and he later allied himself with the French to defeat the Spanish on land in 1658, at the same time capturing Dunkirk. It seemed to be perfectly acceptable for British troops to be fighting for Cromwell with the French and Charles (the King in waiting) with the Spanish.

But feelings among his Parliamentarians were turning against the military dominated regime they had 'voted' in; they wanted to reduce the power of the Council of State and even suggested to Cromwell that he should declare himself King. He agonised for weeks about this but in the end declined, although when he was reinstated he sat on King Edward's throne in ermine robes, and held a sword and sceptre; its regal splendour would not have been lost on anyone. A second chamber of peers was created, dubbed the 'Other House' because the Commons could not agree on a name, but it was effectively a House of Lords. The brief moment of calm soon passed, however, and as opposition rumbled on, Cromwell once again dissolved Parliament in January 1658.

The question remains: What would have happened in England if Cromwell had not died in the following September, probably from a kidney infection but also apparently overcome with grief at the death of his favourite daughter, Elizabeth? Some sort of Parliamentary process had been established with two chambers and there was a degree of peace in England at least. The army had an iron grip on affairs from Scotland to the tip of the West Country, as well as a beaten, if not peaceful, Ireland. But Cromwell was not a well man and he knew he had to consider who would lead the country after him, just as any monarch worried about succession.

Cromwell was 'succeeded' as Lord Protector by his eldest surviving son, Richard, but he did not command the support, or enjoy the power base, of the army that had kept his father secure. Richard resigned as Lord Protector in May 1659, and in the absence of another alternative, the Protectorate was abandoned and the Commonwealth briefly restored. The vacuum left the way clear for George Monck, the English Governor of Scotland, to march south at the head of the New Model Army, reinstate the Long Parliament and in 1660 invite Charles II (1660–1685) home from exile.

There was some unfinished business with Oliver Cromwell, however, as far as the Royalists were concerned. His body was exhumed, posthumously beheaded and displayed on Tyburn Hill, although as in all conspiracy theories there is doubt that it really was his body. Nevertheless, his image lives on in the coins he had minted – including some using a new minting

Charles II

technique introduced by Pierre Blondeau with edge writing to beat forgeries – but above all the monarchy was about to be restored.

Cromwell's legacy and reputation still divides opinion: Was he a regicidal dictator, a military dictator, or a class revolutionary and hero as Leon Trotsky saw him? In Scotland and Ireland where thousands of Catholics suffered under his rule there would be no doubt he was guilty of genocide, and yet in an opinion poll in Britain taken in 2002, he was voted one of the ten greatest Britons of all time.

10 THE RESTORATION

Charles II was in a hurry to make up for lost time. He ascended the throne on 26 May 1660, although all the legal documents show his regnal dates as beginning in 1649, the year his father was executed. He immediately gave orders for new coins to be struck in his name, and of the same type and value as those of his father's reign. When delays occurred he clearly got impatient and reminders were sent out on 18 August and 21 September to the Wardens of the Mint instructing the engraver, Thomas Simon, to get a move on.[72]

The message from Charles was precisely the opposite of previous monarchs who had usurped the throne; it was to re-establish rightful continuity and to obliterate the memory of Cromwell, the Commonwealth, and all talk of republicanism. It was time for the Restoration, bringing the English, Scottish, and Irish monarchies under one King. The message obviously got through because by the end of the year new coinage – including the unite, crown, and double crown – appeared and is regarded by numismatists as some of the finest of the era. The so-called 'Breeches Money' of the Commonwealth was gradually withdrawn.

It was a time of rejoicing and change; change also for the way coins were produced. For just two years the standard 'hammered coins' continued to appear until Pierre Blondeau was invited back to England and his 'modern' milling technique was adopted. This was also the time for the appearance of Britannia on coins. On the reverse of the farthing, for example, the image of Britannia, with which everyone is familiar, is shown with the inscription: QVATOR MARIAVINDICO ('I claim the four seas'). No doubt about who was now in charge, although Charles was to have his own disagreements with Parliament.

72 www.britnumsoc.org

One post-Restoration practice which continues to this day is that the direction in which the monarch is facing changes with each different monarch.

When Charles was invited back to claim his throne, in all the celebration some crucial details had been conveniently or inadvertently overlooked: there was the issue of the powerful army and who actually controlled it, there were unresolved questions about religion, and, as ever, the thorny matter of the King's income. This last point should have been dealt with by Parliament agreeing to pay Charles up to £1.2 million per annum; unfortunately, there always seemed to be a shortfall of about £400,000 which would lead to difficulties.

To understand Charles requires returning to his flight into exile after the Battle of Worcester, or more particularly his escape from England, now remembered in the Monarch's Way 615 mile footpath that zig-zags from Worcester to Shoreham-by-Sea. Quite simply Charles would not have made it, despite his disguises, his hiding in an oak tree, and his masquerading as a humble servant, without the support of many Catholic families hiding him in priest holes and guiding him safely passed Cromwell's troops at great risk to their own lives. When he was at his lowest ebb, with cuts to his feet and exhausted, at a safe house in Moseley, he is quoted as saying to a Catholic priest, Father John Huddleston, who was on his knees bathing the King's feet: 'If it please God I come to my crown, both you and all your persuasion shall have as much liberty as any of my subjects.' He would try to keep to his word but it would be another struggle. While Charles was inclined to tolerate all religions, indeed wanted to formalise the acceptance of practising Catholics, Parliament remained vehemently opposed, despite the Declaration of Breda in April 1660 issued while Charles was still in exile, which as well as granting a general pardon for crimes committed during the civil war, also allowed for the 'liberty of tender consciences' when it came to religion. But it was one thing to make such pronouncements while in exile, or for Parliament to go along with them, it was quite another when it came to enacting them in law. Furthermore, the country was even divided about the direction of the Church of England itself;

new groups had developed during the Commonwealth such as Quakers, Baptists, and Presbyterians. Charles himself was inclined to be tolerant when it came to religious matters; he was more interested in theatre and science, founding the Royal Society.

However, all debating and warfare were brought to an abrupt halt with the outbreak of the Great Plague in 1665, which killed up to 100,000 people – a quarter of London's population. The King and his court left first for Salisbury, and when an outbreak occurred there, to Oxford. Parliament also relocated to Oxford. Those who could escape to their country estates or families did so, the rest had no choice but to remain; it was even forbidden to leave London without a 'clean bill of health' from a doctor – if you could find one who had not fled. Everyone was fearful of contagion and even the exchange of coins was regarded as a risk. In some towns stone crosses can still be seen with a depression at the foot of the cross. This was where they poured vinegar in which to 'cleanse' the coins of any infection. The Council of Scotland voted to ban all trade with England which inevitably led to the loss of many jobs; not only did people not want to exchange money, they didn't even dare risk handling the goods they might otherwise have bought. Businesses closed as the wealthy merchants escaped to the country. It was a brutal time where people often thought only of themselves, quickly throwing servants and even family members out on to the street when they became ill. Samuel Pepys, the diarist who chose to remain in London throughout, noted: '...the plague is making us cruel as dogs to one another...'

By February 1666, the King and his court had returned to London, and it was not long before the city was getting back to normal; people found work easily after so many had died, leaving positions vacant. But London, of course, had more to come when the Great Fire broke out in Pudding Lane the following September; it did not stop the plague, which had already subsided, but it did lead to a great rebuilding using stone rather than wood, and wider streets and better sanitation.

On the one hand, London was booming thanks to extensive rebuilding work after the fire, but economically the country was in trouble. Trade had suffered as a result of the Plague, and the country was also engaged in a second war with the Dutch (1665–1667), who were supported by the French.[73] The country according to Pepys was 'mad for war,' but this time the English were caught napping, and in the final encounter, the Dutch simply broke through the defences guarding the Medway, attacked the fleet at anchor in Chatham Docks and sailed away with the English flagship, the *Royal Charles*. With the Dutch navy now dominant in the seas around England, trade suffered, and Charles was essentially bankrupt. Short of funds and without the backing of Parliament to grant any more, there was no alternative but to sign a peace treaty with the Dutch.

Someone had to be blamed, and Charles pointed the finger at his Lord Chancellor, Lord Clarendon, whom he dismissed and replaced with a group of advisers: Sir Thomas Clifford, Lord Ashley, the Duke of Buckingham, Lord Arlington, and Lord Lauderdale from which we have the derogatory acronym CABAL. Their real role was to try to influence Parliament towards the King's way of thinking, although in practice they never operated together in the real sense of a cabal and indeed failed to achieve their purpose. But this was Charles's style of rule, appointing ministers then dismissing or undermining them, never trusting Parliament, and eventually he decided to rule without it as an absolute monarchy. He avoided unpopular tax raising initiatives by allying with foreign supporters.

Charles's reign is not unique in the number of deals he struck with the motive, sometimes hidden, sometimes obvious, of trying to improve the financial straits in which he found himself. He looked overseas for some solutions. His marriage to the Portuguese princess Catherine of Braganza, for example, won for England Tangier in North Africa and the Seven Islands of Bombay (the beginnings of the British Empire and later the British East India Company)[74] and, among other dowry benefits, the equivalent of £300,000. Charles also raised another £375,000 by selling Dunkirk

---

73 The national debt for 1666-1667 stood at £2.5 million – Christopher Kennedy, *Evolution of Great World Cities: Urban Wealth and Economic Growth*.

74 In 1970 the British East India Company, as well as being granted the right to command its own troops and wage war and acquire new territory, was permitted to mint its own money.

off to his cousin King Louis XIV of France. His best-kept secret was contained hidden away in the terms of the Treaty of Dover in which Louis would pay Charles £160,000 a year and in return Charles would supply France with troops, and secretly promised to convert to Catholicism when the time was most opportune. It is unclear whether he really intended to do this, although it is said that he converted on his deathbed, but no-one knows for sure.

One dark chapter of Charles's reign and desire to search out new business was the rapidly expanding slave trade. In 1672 he granted the Royal African Company a monopoly for a time, but such was the potential profit that Parliament later rescinded the order under pressure from leading merchants. They shipped goods to West Africa where they were exchanged for slaves who were then transported to the vast plantations in America and the Caribbean. Once loaded with a cargo of cotton, tobacco, and sugar the ships returned to Britain.

Charles had managed to sidestep Parliament's reluctance to release funds by borrowing heavily from British goldsmiths, The London Goldsmiths Company, eventually reaching a 10% interest rate. Charles re-introduced the practice of tally sticks first used during the reign of Henry I to keep track of loans. But such was the parlous state of the country's finances in 1672 – not helped by another war with the Dutch – that the monarchy could not honour its debts, and on 2 January the so-called Great Stop of the Exchequer was announced when the Crown halted all debt repayments. For one year interest only was paid and as a result many banks, bankers, and investors went bankrupt. The Goldsmiths Company sued and won, only for the judgement to be overturned by the Lord Chancellor; Charles was presumably advised that in fact usury was against the law and interest rates of more than 6% could not be enforced. The tally sticks were exactly what they were – just worthless sticks, although Charles apparently later regretted the decision as 'a false step'.

As a result of the mismanagement of finances during Charles's reign, in large part due to the fractured relationship between King and Parliament, today we now have the Bank of England, which received its Royal Charter on 27 July 1694. Its role was to raise and lend money to the state and one of the privileges it received in return was the authority to issue bank notes. Never again would the British Government fail to pay its debts.[75] That was all still to come; however, the new financial order can be traced directly back to this period in history. The origin of the word bank itself may be traced to old Norse *bakki* meaning bench or possibly old Italian *banca* meaning table. Whichever is right, we have become familiar with money lenders dispensing largesse in exchange for their pound of flesh, whether they are seated on benches at their green cloth-covered tables in days of yore or in their glittering towers of the 21st century.

Early bank note issued by Bank of England

Parliament, even when dominated by the Cavaliers, remained suspicious about Charles's inclination to show tolerance towards the Catholics, such as through his Declaration of Indulgence, which he was forced to withdraw in 1673. Parliament countered this assertion in the same year with the Test Act, prohibiting Catholics from Public Office, which instantly revealed a new issue: the King's brother, James, had converted to Catholicism.

Now there was the problem of a suitable successor. Catherine had failed to produce any legitimate heirs, although the 'Merry

Monarch' had 14 acknowledged illegitimate children, which left the prospect of James, a Catholic, ascending the throne. Various attempts by Parliament to pass the Exclusion Bill preventing James from becoming King were foiled by the simple expedient of dissolving Parliament again.

Charles died aged 54 and his brother became King James II of England and James VII of Scotland (1685–1689). Initially it was regarded as a smooth succession, but it wasn't long before one of Charles's illegitimate sons, James Scott, the 1st Duke of Monmouth, tried to whip up a rebellion against him, encouraged by William, the Dutch Prince of Orange who had married Mary, King James's daughter by his first marriage to the Protestant commoner Anne Hyde. In a coordinated attack Monmouth and the Earl of Argyll sailed from Holland. Argyll landed in Scotland and was quickly defeated, while Monmouth's army was soundly beaten at the Battle of Sedgemoor on 6 July 1685. Monmouth managed to escape briefly but was captured and taken to London for trial and execution. His supporters were hauled before Judge Jeffreys, presiding in bullying fashion over the so-called 'Bloody Assizes' in Taunton, and were either transported abroad or executed. Those soldiers loyal to the King who were wounded were among the first to be cared for in the newly established Royal Hospital Chelsea.

James II

Despite these initial victories, at the very least James II must have felt nervous; he had successfully seen off the threat from Monmouth and Argyll, but a greater danger was lurking in the shape of a Parliament and a country that were openly hostile to his beliefs.

Ostensibly it was business as usual, with coins being minted in his name, but James was pushing for the Test Act to be repealed and Parliament was having none of it. He was quite obviously too close to France. His second marriage to the Catholic Italian Princess, Mary of Modena, must surely have made his preference clear to all, but the birth of his son, James Stuart (later 'the Old Pretender'), finally set alarm bells ringing about the potential of a Catholic dynasty. James also maintained a standing army, suggesting that he fully intended to fight if necessary to have his way, and made the point by dismissing dissenting Protestant judges and other senior figures in political and academic circles and replacing them with Catholics.

A group of seven notable Englishmen[76] – dubbed the Immortal Seven – wrote to William of the House of Orange-Nassau in the Netherlands inviting him to invade, which William agreed to do so on the understanding that he would be made King in James's place; he didn't just want to be Prince Consort to his wife Mary. The Glorious Revolution was about to begin.

In November 1688 a powerful Dutch force helped by good weather (the Protestant Wind), landed in Brixham, where they faced little opposition; senior Protestant officers led by Lord Churchill of Eyemouth, later the 1st Duke of Marlborough, who had fought against Monmouth, quickly began to defect. James fled to France in December, and in March 1689 he sailed with a force of French soldiers to Ireland, where he had strong Catholic backing.

Unfortunately for James, the Irish had seen this conflict coming and large quantities of gold and silver had either been sent by Protestants to England for safekeeping, or it was being hoarded. Once again a king was short of money to finance his war, and with a dysfunctional government there was no alternative way of raising new taxes. To get round this James announced that a new mint would be established in Dublin,

> ...for the remedy of the present scarcity of money, and that our standing forces may be better paid, and that our subjects of this realm may be better enabled to pay and discharge the taxes, excise, customs, rents, and other debts and duties, which are or shall be hereafter payable to us...

The Irish emergency currency with sixpenny pieces in copper and brass was issued and anyone refusing to accept the new coinage would be 'punished according to the utmost rigour

---

76 The seven were: The Earls of Danby, Shrewsbury and Devonshire, Viscount Lumley, the Bishop of London (Henry Compton), Edward Russell, and Henry Sydney.

of the law'.[77] The sixpenny pieces were soon
followed by brass half crowns and shillings,
but James faced a new problem: Ireland was
simply running out of brass, and it was even
necessary to melt down church bells and two
old guns from Dublin Castle – 'Gunmoney'
was official.

Gunmoney

As far as James was concerned this was all a
temporary measure and as soon as the conflict
was over the coins, which had markings to denote
the month of issuance, could be redeemed for gold
or silver. To begin with this arrangement worked well,
until brass started running low. Desperate appeals were sent to
France, including to Queen Mary who had sought refuge there,
asking first for brass or even cannons which could be melted down,
as well as troops to support the Jacobite cause. The French soldiers
did arrive but they insisted on being paid in gold or silver, which
some suggest led to people refusing to accept the brass coinage as
legitimate tender; merchants began hoarding items which they felt
might have had a greater long-term value than the brass currency.
Even pewter was used in 1690 with a central brass plug to produce
half crowns and crowns, as well as tin for farthings again with a
copper plug which discouraged forgery.

Of course, the crisis was not temporary. James was caught
trying to flee England but allowed to escape by William to
demonstrate that he had abandoned his throne rather than allow
him to be seen as a martyr. Both Houses of Parliament agreed
on 13 February 1689, by the Declaration of Right, that the throne
was vacant and, under pressure from William, who wanted to be
crowned in his own right and not just as Mary's consort, their
joint coronation took place at Westminster Abbey on 11 April,
controversially by the Bishop of London, Henry Compton. The
Archbishop of Canterbury, William Sancroft, refused to perform
the ceremony claiming the removal of James was illegal and the
coronation therefore 'a popish mockery'. In December, William

77 D. Stevenson, www.britnumsoc.org

agreed to a tough new Bill of Rights, which among many other restrictions excluded Roman Catholics, as well as those who married Roman Catholics, from ascending the throne. It was not until 2013 (Succession to the Crown Act) that this restriction was lifted.

However, there was still the matter of the Catholic rebellion in Ireland to be dealt with, where James was holding out and still claiming he was the legitimate King of three nations. William sent a strong force to oppose him but progress was slow, even though support among the locals was waning as local farmers were more inclined to sell their produce to the Williamite troops in return for real money rather than to be paid in brass by the Jacobites. Finally, William himself sailed over to lead his troops and defeated James at the Battle of the Boyne on 1 July 1690. James fled once more to France where he would later die in exile in 1701, but that battle remains a scar on Anglo-Irish relations to this day, dividing the Protestant north from the Catholic south, with Orange Order parades taking place every year on 12 July to celebrate William's victory.

There were two other important consequences of the fighting in Ireland. One: by involving the French, England inexorably would now be drawn into a hundred years of war in Europe. Two: Parliament now had control of an expensive fighting machine which would help build the Empire.

11 TO THE HANOVERIAN SUCCESSION

The reign of William III (1689–1702) and Mary II (1689–1694) was an accommodation on various levels which seemed to suit everyone, and we have the coins of the two monarchs together in harmony. Mary did not think much of her cousin, William, when it was first suggested by her uncle, Charles II, that the two should marry, but she did marry him, despite being 12 years his junior; apparently she was in tears throughout the wedding ceremony.[78] As far as William was concerned it made complete political sense, uniting England and the Netherlands against Catholic France and its desires to dominate Europe. In time they came to love one another in their own way despite William's long-running affair with Elizabeth Villiers, one of Mary's ladies-in-waiting. William is reported to have said as Mary lay dying from smallpox that he 'had never known a single fault in her'.[79]

William and Mary

There was also an accommodation by Parliament who really only wanted Mary as Queen, but William made it clear that he would simply pull his troops out and leave England to fight on alone against the Jacobites unless he was King in his own right. Mary too said she would only return to England as Queen if they sat on the throne together. As it turned out both would have their own way, as William spent much of his time overseas at war leaving Mary to rule in his absence, always taking her husband's advice. Mary was not afraid to take tough decisions herself though, even sending her own uncle, Henry Hyde, to prison for trying to put James II back on the throne. When William was in England, Mary withdrew from politics leaving the

---

78 *The House of Stuart: William III and Mary II* (English Monarchs, 2004).

79 *Cobbett's Parliamentary History of England: From the Norman Conquest*

King to take charge. Everyone was happy: Mary was popular and much loved; William was tolerated and often abroad.

Parliament now had a strong grip on the King's expenditure, making him entirely dependent on his ministers; one, Sir Joseph Williamson, said, 'When princes have not needed money, they have not needed us'.[80] However, it clearly saw no reason at first not to give him free rein to pursue the Jacobite rebels in Scotland, and then to devote years to the defeat of Louis XIV, who had revoked the Edict of Nantes in 1685. No sooner had he ascended the throne then William took the country into the League of Augsburg, later the Grand Alliance, which included at times the Holy Roman Empire, Holland, Spain, Portugal, Sweden, and various anti-German states. It was initially formed to protect the Electorate of the Palatinate, part of the Holy Roman Empire on the Rhine, from Louis's expansionist ideas. The fighting was a combination of siege warfare by land and occasional sea battles. It did not always go England's way and for a time the French navy was dominant, causing some to write to James II saying they were considering joining him. The English suffered a heavy defeat at the Battle of Beachy Head in 1690, when for once Queen Mary took command and overruled her admiral, Arthur Herbert, 1st Earl of Torrington, ordering him to attack the vastly superior French fleet.

It took the destruction of an English village by the French to strengthen the doubters' resolve and the French were themselves defeated in a major naval battle at La Hogue in 1692, once and for all giving the English navy command of the seas.

The Alliance would fight on until 1697, when Louis agreed to give up much of the land he had conquered, only to resume again with the War of Spanish Succession[81] which continued until 1714.

England was preoccupied with Europe because, since 1600 and before, it had had its eyes on the trading opportunities further afield in the East, and thanks to its dominant navy, not to mention the entrepreneurial spirit of countless engineers and other

---

80 *Cobbett's Parliamentary History of England: From the Norman Conquest*

81 This war was sparked by the deathbed decision of the childless Charles II of Spain to nominate his grandson, Philip, the Duke of Anjou, to succeed him. But Philip was also the second eldest grandson of Louis XIV which many thought would threaten European stability.

adventurers, an empire was now about to grow. And it is from these adventures that one of the key moments in the country's financial history would occur.

Europe had recognised the potential of the East and, of course, there were fears that the French would try to dominate there. In broad terms the Dutch were focussed on the spice trade and the English largely on textiles, and they each had their own businesses: the East India Company as it became (originally chartered as the 'Governor and Company of Merchants of London trading in the East Indies' because India per se did not yet exist) and the equivalent Dutch East India Company. The French had their own Compagnie des Indes Orientales, established in 1664.

Crucially, the English learned some important lessons about managing their finances from the Dutch who

> introduced the English to a number of key financial institutions that the Dutch had pioneered. One result was that the Bank of England was founded in 1694 using the Dutch model to manage the government's borrowings and the national currency. A system of national public debt was funded by the stock exchange, and the apparatus for low-interest borrowing became a reality for the British government.[82]

Frankly there was no alternative because William's 'credit rating' was so poor it was impossible to raise the £1.2 million needed to rebuild the navy.

On 27 July 1694 William Paterson, a Scottish merchant, was granted the Royal Charter to establish the Bank of England to raise money for the Government. The lenders gave the bank bullion and in return were issued with bank notes which were handwritten. The money was raised within 12 days, and half of it was used to rebuild the navy.

As Parliament strengthened its place at the centre of Government, in 1697 William appointed a group of ministers drawn from the majority Whigs in the House of Commons, who would meet regularly outside Parliament essentially as managers

82 Kartar Lalvani, *The Making of India: The Untold Story* (Bloomsbury, 2016).

working on the King's behalf; the concept, if not the reality, of the Cabinet system was born.

The quality of coins was again a problem and in 1696 'An Act for Remedying the Ill State of Coins' was passed. It would prove to be a costly business in itself, some £2.7 million, and as usual the poor suffered most, failing to redeem their clipped coins in time. Mints around the country were working flat out and the cost of the process was met by a tax on windows – the Act of Enlightenment. Not everyone got enough of the new money and in Ireland workers were paid in 'promissory cards,' signed on the back, to be exchanged for cash at a later date.

One other impediment, which for so long had blighted relations between monarch and Parliament, was also removed in 1698 with the introduction of the Civil List, which granted the Sovereign income to manage his or her household and the cost of civil government. War was an expensive business, and to meet the annual £5 million cost the Land Tax was brought in, taxing rents and produce of the land.

The question of succession was becoming an issue because William was not a healthy man, suffering constantly from a lung disease, and Mary had failed to produce an heir. In 1701 the Act of Settlement was passed which not only fixed Parliament at the centre of running the country's affairs and restricting the King from going to war, but also precluded Catholics from the throne or monarchs from marrying a Catholic.

William never recovered after falling from his horse, which stumbled into a mole's hole, and he died in 1702; Jacobites immediately toasted 'the little gentleman in the black velvet waistcoat'. With no other suitable heirs, the crown passed to Mary's sister Anne (1702–1714).

Even before she ascended the throne, Anne was a sick woman, but during her 12 year reign she managed to accomplish at least one important feat: the union of the country as Great Britain, marked, of course, by a new coin. But the time leading up to her coronation was physically difficult.

Suitable candidates for succession must have been a constant subject for debate in royal circles as one by one those directly in line died prematurely. Anne's marriage to her second cousin once removed, Prince George of Denmark – specifically arranged to limit Dutch power and influence, something which was not likely to endear him to William III – resulted in 17 pregnancies, the last in 1700. But all of her children miscarried, were still born or died young; the longest surviving child, Prince William, Duke of Gloucester, died at the age of 11.

As for George, he just wanted a quiet time; he hated court life, was regularly snubbed by William's supporters and even endured delays in the payment of his allowance. Anne was persuaded not to ask Parliament to make him King Consort.

However, matters were anything but quiet for Anne and her ministers. The War of Spanish Succession had begun following the death of Charles II of Spain without an heir, sparking the acquisitive ambitions of France to unite the two countries under one, Catholic, monarch. There were two camps: the Habsburg Archduke Charles of Austria and the Bourbon Philip, Duke of Anjou. Just two months after Anne's coronation, England entered the war alongside Austria and the Netherlands.

One early encounter by the English to try and capture Cadiz was a failure, but this was 'spun' into a success story when the navy intercepted Franco-Spanish ships laden with gold and silver treasure sailing back from America at the Battle of Vigo Bay, in October 1702. Among the coins minted from the gold were five guinea 'Vigo' coins. The coin shows the profile of Queen Anne, already looking quite portly, with the word VIGO beneath her bust, and on the reverse four shields with the arms of England, Scotland, Ireland, and France. Anne ruled that the word VIGO, '...under our effigies, which inscription we intend as a mark of distinction from the rest of our gold and silver moneys to continue to posterity the remembrance of that glorious action.'[83] Cadiz itself was to be forgotten. There are probably only 20 left in existence and when a 'lost' five guinea coin, found in a private collector's desk by his widow, came up for auction in Tunbridge Wells, Kent, in 2012 it sold for £300,000.

83 Royal warrant, 10 February 1703.

Anne – VIGO coin

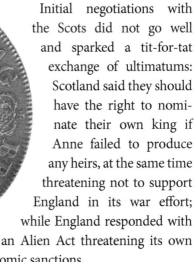

Anne's weight was an issue; she was suffering from gout and found it difficult walk. Even at her coronation she had to be carried into Westminster Abbey in a sedan chair. The designers of the Vigo coins were probably flattering, but Anne pressed on with her work and she was crystal clear as to what her prime objective would be: the union of the kingdom.

Initial negotiations with the Scots did not go well and sparked a tit-for-tat exchange of ultimatums: Scotland said they should have the right to nominate their own king if Anne failed to produce any heirs, at the same time threatening not to support England in its war effort; while England responded with an Alien Act threatening its own economic sanctions.

Finally, in 1707, both sides backed down and the Act of Union bringing England and Scotland together as Great Britain was signed. It was marked with a change in coinage reflecting the union: on the five guinea coin the English and Scottish lions appear on the two shields and on the reverse the rose was replaced by the Garter Star. Weights and measure would be standardised and coins would be recognised on both sides of the border in a common currency introduced under the auspices of Sir Isaac Newton, then Master of the Mint.

No sooner had Anne been celebrating this success then disaster struck once more at sea: four Royal Navy warships sank off the coast of Sicily due to a navigational error, with a loss of 1,550 sailors. Prince George as Lord High Admiral was nominally responsible and there were demands for him to step down, but worse was to follow. George, who had a lung disease, possibly asthma, fell ill the following year and died in October leaving Anne inconsolable, although the rest of the court seemed unmoved. He had always been regarded as dull and ineffectual; mocking his asthma, John Sheffield, the Duke of Buckingham and Lord Privy Seal, said he was forced to breathe hard in case people thought he was dead and buried him.

When Anne herself died in 1714, her nearest Protestant relative was George, Elector of Hanover and the eldest son of the Duke of Brunswick-Luneberg and his wife, Sophia, who was the granddaughter of King James I through her mother, Elizabeth of Bohemia. He was a distant 52nd in line to throne compared with the many closer Catholic contenders, but they were ineligible due to the Act of Settlement. It was time to usher in the House of Hanover and the Georgian Era.

The truth is George I (1714–1727) was a convenient monarch for Britain. Nobody particularly liked the pale, slight German, who had locked up his wife, Sophia, for adultery back in Hanover, and arrived in the country with his two mistresses: one mocked as a 'maypole,' the other as an 'elephant'. The writer, William Thackeray, said their motive was to 'take what you can' from Britain,[84] about which the old King, 54 when he came to throne, seemed to have little interest. An attempt was even made to control the King's wardrobe expenditure with an arbitrary figure of £18,000 being set but never met.[85]

George spoke German and French but little English, which seemed to suit the dominant Whig party well. They had won an overwhelming victory in the 1715 election and ministers were left largely to their own devices, running the country during the King's

---

84 William Thackeray, *The Four Georges*.

85 John Beattie, *The English Court in the Reign of George 1* (Cambridge University Press, 1967).

many absences visiting his beloved Hanover. In Hanover he was an absolute monarch in charge of all expenditure and official appointments; in Britain he had to listen to Parliament.

Coins were promptly minted firmly to establish George's legitimate right to the throne, as in 1715 he faced immediate rebellion from the Jacobites, supported by some Tories, who wanted to see James Stuart, Anne's Roman Catholic half-brother, on the throne. The rebellion was short-lived but the cause had not gone away. Without funds, men, or the backing of the French following the death of Louis XIV, the claims of the Old Pretender evaporated and the Tories were cast into the political wilderness for the next half-century.

George I

George's apparent lack of interest in Britain effectively marked the consolidation of the Cabinet system we have today with a 'Prime' Minister at its head. The first man to hold that position in all but name was Sir Robert Walpole, whose administration would last, with one brief break in 1716–1717, until 1742.

In fact, more recent assessments of George's rule point to a man who, far from being wooden and dull-witted, was perfectly able to communicate in French with his ministers and positively influenced foreign policy, forging strategic alliances in Europe. This suited Walpole, who resisted all arguments to go to war, preferring always to focus on business and commercial opportunities in order to maintain peace. During the Sovereign's regular absences to attend to business in Hanover, rather than leave his son, George, the Prince of Wales, whom he positively disliked, in charge, authority rested with a Regency Council, but Walpole was running the country. Furthermore, with the passing of the Septennial Act in 1716 the life of every Parliament was now extended from three to seven years; another way of ensuring continuity of policy and, as a consequence, prosperity.

Britain and the nature of work were changing. Government and the need for a civil service to continue running affairs as ministers came and went was recognised, the financial industry was growing rapidly, and there was 'a new breed of professionals, money-men, bankers, brokers and stockjobbers, who practised new ways of handling and dealing with financial matters, such as fire insurance and bills of exchange'.[86]

Not every financial deal was a success: in 1720 Parliament passed the South Sea Bill allowing the South Sea Company a monopoly on trade with South America in return for a loan of £7 million. Shares in the company rocketed to ten times their value as speculation and fraud ran riot. Then, of course, the bubble burst and thousands, including it is said the King himself, lost money, and others their life savings and their homes. Walpole's skilful management of the Crown's involvement, deflecting potential embarrassment, secured his position as de facto ruler, being appointed First Lord of the Treasury and Chancellor of the Exchequer in 1721 – in effect the 'Prime' Minister; the constitutional monarchy with a cabinet answering to Parliament, and a Parliament answerable to an electorate was still not formally in place, and the Great Reform Act of 1832 bringing in sweeping changes to the electoral system was still some way off, but the foundations had been laid.

George I died of a stroke on his way for another visit to Hanover and was succeeded by his son, George II (1727–1760), with whom he had finally been reconciled, although the new King would in turn fall out with his own son.

Britain was on the verge of becoming the mightiest empire since Rome and the Industrial Revolution was almost upon us, but

86 Strong, *The Story of Britain*.

despite Walpole's best efforts there were seemingly endless wars to be fought and victories to be won, which were duly marked in new coins.

George had three great loves: his wife, music, and the army. Indeed, during the War of Austrian Succession, he became the last Sovereign to lead his forces into battle. It was a close-run thing for a while when the British, together with the Austrians and Hanoverians, met the French forces at Dettingen on the River Main in Germany on 27 June 1743. George himself might have been captured were it not for an impulsive attack by the French cavalry which was repelled, allowing the 'Pragmatic Army'[87] to escape a potential trap.

George's first great love, of course, was his wife, Caroline of Ansbach, who persuaded her husband to retain Walpole rather than replace him with Sir Stephen Compton, recognising that Walpole enjoyed the support of the majority in Parliament. It was a wise decision, as Walpole found himself constantly trying to dissuade George from getting involved with every European conflict that arose.

To begin with there was quite enough distraction at home when Charles Edward Stuart, 'Bonnie Prince Charlie', son of the Old Pretender, landed in Scotland and once again tried to raise support for the Jacobite cause. After an initial victory at the Battle of Prestonpans in August 1745 against loyalist troops, the Jacobites then came up against George's son, Prince William, and his mixed army including Hessians from Germany, Austrians, Ulstermen, and even some Lowland Scots, who routed them at Culloden on 16 April 1746 after the French failed to provide enough support. Bonnie Prince Charlie managed to escape to France and all hopes of a return for the House of Stuart were over.

Britain's navy continued to grow, win victories, and bring home treasure. In July 1745 two privateers captured two French ships loaded with bullion returning from Callao, the port of Lima. When they reached Bristol it took 45 wagons to carry the silver

---

87 Pragmatic Army was a group of states supporting the Pragmatic Sanction, an edict proclaimed by Charles VI permitting a daughter to inherit the Hapsburg Empire's territories.

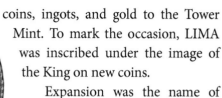

coins, ingots, and gold to the Tower Mint. To mark the occasion, LIMA was inscribed under the image of the King on new coins.

Expansion was the name of the game, with the dual purpose of bringing political power and vast wealth to Britain; the Mercantile System held sway, which essentially was the export of British goods for foreign currency as opposed to the purchase of foreign goods for British money. The Government and the merchants were working in parallel: as the merchants grew wealthy, the Treasury's coffers swelled through taxation. Among the adventurers growing rich and enjoying the complete support of the government was Robert Clive – 'Clive of India'.

LIMA, George II

When this soldier of fortune was sent to India in 1744, merely as an agent of the East India Company (EIC), he found only a small base at Fort St George near what is now Madras. The India at the time was a multitude of semi-independent princely states within the Mughal Empire. Competing with the EIC, initially just for commercial dominance, were the Dutch, the French, and the Portuguese. The focus gradually changed as each group developed armed forces to protect their interests and territory:

Initially these commercial enterprises were uninterested in territory and concerned only with profits, but once invested in new areas, they wanted more stability and control. The European powers, meanwhile, wanted to keep rival countries out. Thus began the land grabs and construction of formal empires, of which Britain's grew to become the largest.[88]

Gold coins struck from the booty sent home by the EIC bear the company's initials.

The EIC had been sending bullion to a mint in Surat since 1621, during the reign of James I, where they were turned into gold mohurs and silver rupees. Eventually, in 1672, the EIC opened its own mint on the island of Bombay, producing European style coins in gold, silver, copper, and even tin with the company's arms and the inscription HON:SOC:ANG:IND:ORI ('The Honourable East India Company').

Thanks to the betrayal by the Indian army chief, Mir Jafar, Clive achieved his greatest victory at the Battle of Plassey in 1757, defeating 50,000 troops of the Nawab of Bengal, supported by his French allies, with a force of just 3,200. It made him the undisputed master, and virtual ruler, of India's richest province, Bengal. Over the next 100 years, the EIC would come to rule over much of the rest of the country. But, as Dr. Kartar Lalvani writes in his book, *The Making of India*, Britain's relationship with India was a two way street:

> There were, however, two sides to British rule: one was commercial and at times severely exploitative, particularly under the early rule of the East India Company, a private trading monopoly; the other was liberal and that liberalism was high minded and enduring in its benefaction, with a legacy and feats of public works that remain unparalleled today. Such liberalism meshed with the deep roots of Indian culture that is peaceful and harmonious. [89]

In Europe, France had been fighting sporadic skirmishes with Britain since 1754 – the Seven Years War – but all-out war

88 Zakaria, *The Post-American World* .
89 Lalvani, *The Making of India*.

was formally declared in 1756 when France attacked Prussia, a British ally. The French planned a knock-out blow by invading Britain with a force of 100,000 troops in 1759. The invasion never happened due to a series of French defeats, first in summer 1759 at Port Lagos as the French fleet tried to slip through a blockade out of the Straits of Gibraltar, and then at the Battle of Quiberon Bay, where the main invasion force was gathered. A diversionary manoeuvre sending five ships to Ireland to garner Jacobite support ended in disaster when the French squadron was caught and sunk in the Irish Channel.

Meanwhile, British international trade received another boost when, in 1759 Major General James Wolfe led a combined British and American force against the French and Canadians to capture Quebec. Wolfe died from his wounds at the Battle of the Plains of Abraham but was hailed as the hero and architect of the victory which ultimately led to the capture of Montreal leading to British rule in Canada.

When George died suddenly he was succeeded by his grandson, George III (1760–1820), his own son, Frederick, having predeceased him in 1751. Officially, George III was King of

George III

Great Britain and Ireland; it would not be until 1801 that he became King of a United Great Britain and Ireland. In 1761 George married Charlotte of Mecklinburg-Strelitz and they had 14 children together.

The problem for Britain was, in her eagerness to extract maximum taxes from her burgeoning colonies and not considering for a moment those colonies' right to have a say in the level of taxes imposed, stirred up resentment. At the end of the Seven Years War, effectively driving France out of America, a Stamp Tax, for example, was imposed, forcing the colonies to pay for the pensions of the British officers who had actually defeated them. Resentment grew into protests – the Boston Tea Party, for example – then into the full-scale Revolutionary War, when 13 of the colonies declared themselves to be the independent United States of America on 4 July 1776. France, still smarting from its defeat in the Seven Years War, signed an alliance with the Americans in 1778, marking the start of the Anglo-French War.

Over the coming years, Britain found herself fighting multiple opponents in different parts of the world: the Spanish and the Dutch backed the American revolutionaries, supplying them with weapons; in India the EIC launched an attack against French outposts when they heard France had entered the war; Spain also joined in the fighting in 1779 in a bid to capture Gibraltar and Minorca, and there were even naval skirmishes between France and Britain in the West Indies.

Just as in America, where new and higher taxes sparked revolution, so too in France; with the largest population in Europe (29 million), the constant fighting in the 18th century had to be paid for, and the people, suffering from severe crop failures, wanted change, they wanted a greater say in how they were governed, and, fatally, the monarchy was no longer held in awe.

How was all this reflected in the coins of Britain? France was perceived as a real and growing threat, and the widespread nature of the conflict would soon prove to be a strain on the economy. The French Revolution (1787–1799) was about to grip France and a new financial crisis was about to hit America and Britain.

First, tensions between France and Britain rose; the French ambassador was thrown out of the country following the execution of Louis XVI, and on 1 February 1793, France declared war in response, swiftly raising a vast army.

In America, the property bubble burst in 1796, eventually bringing down many leading firms and figures, including the likes of Robert Morris, who had largely financed the Revolution, and James Wilson, one of the signatories to the Declaration of

Independence. The panic in American credit markets soon spread to Britain, where people were also alarmed by talk of a French invasion, and began emptying their accounts. In February 1797, the Bank of England stopped issuing gold and instead made payment in banknotes, which became legal tender for the first time, or silver coins. There was even the ignominy of stamping the King's image onto foreign coins, and Spanish eight *reales* (pieces of eight) – the currency of the enemy – were widely accepted.

The British economy had suffered as a result of bankrolling others such as Austria, Prussia, and Russia to fight in the French Revolutionary and Napoleonic Wars on its behalf. Trade had also inevitably been hit as France retaliated by cutting off European markets for British products. Coins were in short supply. Some mining companies and businesses issued their own copper 'tokens' which inevitably were met with some distrust. One moneyer, Matthew Boulton, was permitted to strike his own coins at his Soho Mint in Birmingham, dubbed the 'Cartwheel' pennies because of their size.

The much vaunted invasion by the French of course never happened following Admiral Nelson's victory at Trafalgar in 1803, although the King himself had been ready for the fight as he wrote to his friend, Bishop Hurd: 'We are in daily expectation that Bonaparte will attempt his threatened invasion. Should his troops affect a landing, I shall certainly put myself at the head of mine, and my other armed subjects, to repel them.'

The European threat, however, had not gone away. Various coalitions against France were formed, ranging from Austria, Prussia, and Spain to the Ottoman Empire, only to fall away either through separate peace treaties or defeat. For a time Britain stood alone with no allies against Napoleon Bonaparte until finally, with growing unrest about Napoleon's ambitions, Austria, Russia, and Prussia (the Seventh Coalition) joined the Duke of Wellington's army eventually to defeat Napoleon at the Battle of Waterloo on 18 June 1815.

The King and his people were triumphant and it called for a special coin; in fact, it called for a wholesale re-coinage in 1816 to stabilise the economy. The master Italian engraver, Benedetto

Benedetto Pistrucci design, Gold Sovereign, 1820

Pistrucci, was summoned to court and was commissioned to design new gold and silver coinage. The star turn was his Waterloo Medal and the George and Dragon image on the gold sovereign of 1817, regarded as a numismatic masterpiece.

George had indeed slain the French dragon and the same design was to appear on the gold five pound coins and silver crowns. Only silver coins were produced for general usage; copper pennies were minted exclusively for use in the Botany Bay Penal Colony in Australia.

However, in reality the King was not well, slipping in and out of bouts of insanity, suffering from porphyria; by 1811 it had been agreed that his fun-loving son, George, should become Prince Regent as his father, 'mad King George,' was by then blind and totally insane. George III saw out the final years of his reign in seclusion at Windsor Castle until his death on 29 January 1820.

The King may not have been well but his ministers were working hard on his behalf as the British Empire continued to grow. The British navy had mastery of the seas, and although the American colonies may have been lost, expansion continued around the globe, from Canada to Africa and the East. The Industrial Revolution was in full flight, average income was rising, and the population grew rapidly as a result of people marrying younger and living longer, and better nutrition. There was opposition though from some fearful of the impact of so much 'automation'. The Luddites smashed new weaving machines that were turning the cotton and jute, transforming the textile industry but reducing the demand for labour.

When George IV (1820–1830) ascended the throne, already 57 years old, no-one really expected much from him; indeed he was to be a disappointment to his ministers and his people. His reputation for indulging in high-living and lowly mistresses was well-established; he was obese, addicted to laudanum, and had run up enormous debts. On the plus side, in his youth he was a man of style and wit. He encouraged the arts and architecture, promoting the architect John Nash with his designs for Regent Street and Regent's Park, as well as backing the idea of the extravagant Royal Pavilion at Brighton. He probably enjoyed finally seeing his own face on coins after waiting so long in the wings to succeed his father, but money passed through his hands like water. His own coronation cost some £20 million in today's terms.

George IV

Politically, he was on the margins, as the world about him changed; people became more affluent and in turn more demanding. There was a sniff of revolution in the air with large public meetings and talk of universal male suffrage. In Manchester, mobs protesting against the Corn Laws, which restricted grain imports and pushed up prices, were dispersed by soldiers, and 11 people were killed in the so-called Peterloo Massacre 1819.

There may have been 658 Members of Parliament but it was an open secret that their election was sometimes fraudulent as a result of the 'rotten boroughs' returning MPs on the strength of a handful of votes or a fistful of bribes. Perhaps the biggest political change was the acceptance that Catholics should be recognised as equals, granting them the right to sit in

Parliament under the Roman Catholic Relief Act 1829. By then George had long since retired to Windsor Castle more or less blind, weighing 20 stone, and under the constant care of his physicians.

When he finally died, un-mourned, one anonymous obituary writer said: 'During the later years of his life, a quiet indulgence of certain sensual enjoyments seemed the sole object of his existence.' In short, it was a wasted life which could have produced much more.

He was succeeded by his 64-year-old brother, William IV (1830–1837), whose brief reign was to be dominated by political change, the most notable being the Great Reform Bill 1832 which allowed the burgeoning middle classes – that is, those with property valued for rates at least £10 per annum – to vote. Aristocrats still retained real power but it was seen as a step in the right direction. Two other landmark measures were the abolition of slavery throughout the British Empire in 1833 – although William had spoken against it in the House of Lords when still a Duke, even insulting the abolitionist, William Wilberforce, by name in his speech – and the first Factory Act in the same year, improving conditions for children working in the new factories springing up. It was also the year the Royal Navy, in which as a boy William 'the Sailor King' had served, annexed the Falkland Islands before they became a Crown Colony in 1841; years later this would provoke war between Argentina and Great Britain.

One old form of coinage – the tally stick, unused since 1826 – had one last terrible role to play. In 1834, the Exchequer found itself with two carts of sticks lying unwanted, and instructed the Clerk of Works in Parliament to destroy them. On 16 October he ordered two workmen to burn them in the stoves in the basement of the House of Lords. By 5pm, thinking their work was done and the furnaces safely extinguished, they left for the night only for fire to break out, destroying most of both Houses of Parliament.

Numerous coins were issued during William's short reign, which in part reflects Britain's wide empire: the third farthing was struck for use in Malta, the half farthing for use in Ceylon with the image of a seated Britannia on the reverse and the inscription BRITANNIAR:REX:FID:DE, and the silver three halfpence was

Maundy Money, William IV

issued to be used generally in the colonies. The silver penny was exclusively used for Maundy Money, a symbolic gift to the elderly from the monarch, which continues to this day in recognition of those who have done good works.

William had ten illegitimate children by his mistress the actress, Dorothea Bland, known by her stage name as Mrs. Jordan, but he had no legitimate heirs and was succeeded by his niece, Princess Victoria of Kent.

12 VICTORIA TO GEORGE V

The whole landscape of British life was changing at a dramatic pace. A rural existence had been transformed into an urban one; in 1800 a quarter of the population lived in the cities, but well before the end of Victoria's reign (1837–1901) 80% of the population would be town or city dwellers. Farmers and farm labourers had become traders and shopkeepers, and that meant an enormous increase in demand for coins. In one year 6.7 million penny coins were minted.[90] It was not all wealth and happiness though; housing for the majority, which sprang up to cope with the influx of workers and their families, was grim and unsanitary, tuberculosis was rife, working hours were punishing, and wages inevitably low.

Victoria (young head)

On the other hand, the Empire was expanding until indeed it became one upon which the sun never set; a quarter of the world's population at one point were using British coins. When Victoria came to the throne she was just a young girl of 18. Her youthful face was depicted on the new coins – the Young Head – first issued in 1838 and which continued to be minted for the next 50 years. Her hair is pulled up at the back with a pony tail hanging down, reflecting her youth.

Three years after becoming Queen she married her first cousin, Prince Albert of Saxe-Coburg and Gotha, and together they had nine children. It was a time when anything must have seemed possible

for Victoria; she was supported by the first of ten prime ministers in her reign, Lord Melbourne, and had her husband at her side. Britain was the centre of global trade: 'By 1850 over 90% of exports were of manufactured goods and a quarter of all international trade passed through British ports, mainly in British ships.'[91] Between 1845 and 1870, Britain was producing some 30% of the world's Gross Domestic Product.[92]

To maintain this prosperity and stability, Victoria favoured peaceful settlement whenever possible; her children married into royal and noble families on the Continent creating families ties and earning her the unofficial title 'the grandmother of Europe'. Above all, cementing relations with the old enemy, France, was important, and she became the first British monarch to visit the country since Henry VIII when she and Albert stayed with King Louis Philippe I in Normandy. When Louis Philippe was deposed by the Revolutions of 1848, which spread throughout Europe and momentarily threatened Victoria herself, he sought sanctuary in England.

In a foretaste of what was to follow many years later, in 1847 it was suggested in Parliament that the British currency should be decimalised. The idea was dropped but it was agreed that a coin valued at one tenth should be produced, more or less to test the water and gauge the public's reaction. They argued for a while over the name; centum, decade, and dime were all considered before they settled on florin, dubbed the 'godless florin' because the inscription DG or DEI GRATIA ('By the Grace of God') was omitted. It was redesigned in 1851 with FIDEI DEFENSOR ('Defender of the Faith') restored.

As an indication of the strength of Britain's global reach at the time, the Royal Navy's control ensured the flow of goods from its possessions and colonies continued; it imposed a stranglehold on China, blocking ports and enabling the EIC to push further into the country, introducing opium as a bribe or sweetener in exchange for Chinese goods. In the Opium Wars which followed China was no match for the superior technology of the British;

91 Strong, *The Story of Britain*.
92 Zakaria, *The Post-American World* .

the island of Hong Kong was ceded, and even the tea plants were taken to India where they were found to grow equally well, starting a new industry.

In 1851, when the Great Exhibition was staged in the glittering Crystal Palace in Hyde Park with displays of manufacturing prowess, there could have been little doubt about Britain's standing in the world. Although there were colonial disputes, only the Crimean War (1854–1856) disrupted the reign in Europe, sparked by a threat from Russia to carve up Turkey – 'the sick man of Europe' – which, before long, involved Britain, Austria, France, and Italy. The two most famous battles were Balaklava (the Charge of the Light Brigade) and Inkerman. Florence Nightingale, the Lady of the Lamp, who revolutionised nursing and went with a group of volunteers to care for the injured during the war, was commemorated 150 years later when the £2 silver proof coin was struck in her name. The Victoria Cross was introduced in 1856 to mark acts of bravery during this war.

The first rumblings of discontent in the Empire began in 1857 with the Indian Mutiny when *sepoys*, Indian soldiers recruited by the EIC, rose up, essentially over terms and conditions. Rumours also spread that the cartridges used in the British issue rifles, which had to be bitten to release the powder, were coated in animal fat which would have offended both Hindu and Muslim soldiers. The uprising was put down but the most significant outcome was the transfer of power from the EIC to direct British Government control. The Raj was born, but Victoria wanted it to be a benevolent rule specifically permitting religious tolerance, despite the claims of modern revisionist Indian historians.

EIC Rupee, Victoria

How the matter was actually broached is not known, but someone must have decided that the youthful image of the queen needed 'updating' as the reign wore on, and the slightly older image, the so-called 'bun head', appeared in 1860, and for the first time the value of the coin, one penny, was inscribed on the bronze coin.

Then tragedy struck in 1861 when Prince Albert died and Victoria sank into deep mourning, rarely appearing in public and always dressed in black. Her absence from public life only served to encourage a mood of republicanism, which subsided when her son, the Prince of Wales, became dangerously ill with typhoid, and later when there was an apparent attempt on her life, although the pistol wielded by 17-year-old Irishman Arthur O'Connor was unloaded. He was seized by Victoria's manservant, John Brown, and arrested.

By the mid-1870s Victoria's revered status throughout her Empire was assured; with the passing of the Royal Titles Act in 1874 she took the title 'Empress of India' which now appeared on new coinage.

As the Empire's boundaries expanded, Britain's plans for southern Africa did not run as smoothly. There were conflicts, such as the Anglo-Zulu Wars, forever remembered in the Battle of Rorke's Drift (22 January 1879) when 11 Victoria Crosses were awarded, and the frequently forgotten British defeat at Islandlwana on the same day. When the Colonial Secretary, Lord Carnarvon, suggested a confederation of African States including the annexation of the Boer controlled Transvaal, it sparked the first Boer War (1880–1881).

By the time of Victoria's Diamond Jubilee in 1897 Britain's Empire had peaked. Victoria had become the longest reigning British monarch, and discreetly, recognising the passing of the years no doubt, a new 'Old Head' design by Thomas Brock, also known as the Veiled Head or Widow Head, was produced. Coins, including crowns and gold sovereigns with the new image on the obverse and the familiar Benedetto Pistrucci design of St George slaying the Dragon on the reverse, were minted every year from 1893 until Victoria's death in 1901.

Victoria was the last British monarch of the House of Hanover and was succeeded by her son, Edward VII (1901–1910), of the House of Saxe-Coburg and Gotha.

Having served his long apprenticeship as Prince of Wales, Edward had to curtail his life of entertainment, although his accession to the throne reintroduced some welcome glamour to the dour days which had persisted in court for 40 years since Albert's death.

Edward was King of the United Kingdom and British Dominions and Emperor of India as well as being related to virtually every royal family in Europe; where his mother was regarded as the grandmother of Europe, Edward was its 'uncle'. During his time as Prince of Wales he had travelled extensively, entertained widely, and enjoyed the company of mistresses such as Lily Langtree, although he had married Princess Alexandra of Denmark in 1863 by whom he had had six children. His mother disapproved of his philandering and self-indulgent lifestyle, and blamed his liaison with an actress for Albert's premature death. Despite his indulgence, his private secretary, Sir Francis Knollys, claimed Edward was the first monarch to ascend the throne in credit.[93]

Although ill-prepared, once King, Edward threw himself into the business of state and used his European royal connections to smooth diplomatic difficulties. Britain was a wealthy nation, and

Exotic collection, Edward VII

93 Sir Sidney Lee, *King Edward VII, A Biography* (Amazon. Originally published 1910).

Edward VII, King and Emperor of Uganda

London the financial centre of the world, but in the new Edwardian period of plenty and enjoyment, the country had taken its foot off the economic pedal and America was now more prosperous in terms of GDP. All the endeavour and work ethic of the Victorian era was forgotten by those who had once been the driving force of industry in favour of leisure and country-weekend pursuits.

Reflecting Britain's standing in the world, exotic coins such as the ones from Uganda or the former Nigeria British West Africa can be found; worth one tenth of a penny, it was minted with a hole in the middle so they could be worn in a string round the neck.

Gold sovereigns issued during Edward's reign, and more recently, were internationally recognised and became a universal currency used by Special Forces soldiers in their survival kit in case they needed to buy their way out of trouble. Millions of pounds worth of 'unused' 22 carat coins from the 1990/91 Gulf War in Iraq was controversially sold off in presentation packs by the Ministry of Defence, which some members of the SAS said compromised the regiment's mystique. Even James Bond was portrayed as carrying the sovereigns in his briefcase.

Remembering the battles between past monarchs and their governments about how much they needed to survive, we see that the Civil List allocated Edward £470,000 to run his household, compared with Queen Victoria's £385,000.

The Edwardian Age was a time of considerable artistic, literary, and musical accomplishment; there was Edward Lutyens, W.

Somerset Maugham, and Edward Elgar to name just a few. There were scientific advances and the Wright brothers flew for the first time, and even the 1908 Summer Olympics were held in London. But it was a lull before a terrible storm. Edward's close relationship with European heads of state served the country well; he visited Paris, establishing the Entente Cordiale which still survives today, albeit shakily at times, and he was the first British monarch to visit Russia. However, it was the growing suspicion of his own nephew, Kaiser Wilhelm II of Germany, that the rest of Europe was turning against him which eventually would lead to the Great War and its terrible loss of life.

A brewing economic crisis when the Conservative Lords blocked the Liberal 1909 Budget could not be resolved before Edward died on 6 May 1910. Appropriately perhaps for a fun-loving man, his last words were to say how glad he was that his horse, Witch of the Air, had won a race at Kempton Park that very afternoon.

His second-eldest son, George V (1910–1936), was better prepared for the role destiny had waiting for him than his father had been. When George was born Victoria was still Queen, and he was third in line to the throne so he could not have expected to find himself King. But George's brother, Prince Albert, died in 1892, just six weeks after becoming engaged. It meant George had to leave the Royal Navy, which he had joined aged 18, as he was now heir to the throne. His father made him read state documents to ensure he was ready to assume the responsibilities ahead.

George grew close to his brother's fiancée, Princess Victoria Mary of Teck, in their mutual grief, and a year after Albert's death, they married, becoming Duke and Duchess of York, and in 1901 together travelled throughout the Empire. On his return, with great foresight, he warned in a speech at London's Guildhall that '...the Old Country must wake up if she intends to maintain her old position of pre-eminence in her colonial trade against foreign competitors.'[94]

---

94 Harold Nicholson, *King George V.*

Having ascended the throne, George and Queen Mary travelled to India for the Delhi Durbar to be presented as the Emperor and Empress and where, of course, coins were minted in their name, some causing consternation among the Hindu community. The rupee, half rupee, quarter rupee, two annas and quarter anna depicted George wearing a robe with what was supposed to be a small elephant on it. Unfortunately most people thought it looked more like a pig's snout with short legs. Consequently, most of the 'Pig Rupees' were melted down and a more elephant-like version was introduced.

Back in Britain the Liberal budget question was resolved and the power of the Lords curtailed, preventing them from vetoing a financial bill under threat of flooding the House with new peers to ensure the safe passage of the Bill.

In 1914, war was declared against Germany and George, as cousin of Kaiser Wilhelm II, was made to feel uncomfortable about his Germanic connections, not to mention his own name. In 1917, by royal proclamation he changed the name of the royal household to Windsor and he and his family dropped all their German titles.

War also had a direct impact on the coins. Due to a sharp increase in the price of silver, the mint reduced the silver value of all new coins issued after 1919, and this value continued for another 26 years. The same effect was felt overseas, such as in India where the silver half rupee and 2 annas were discontinued and replaced with cupro-nickel coins. These were not popular and assumed to be of little value, so later silver coins came back into circulation.

While the monarch was by now clearly only supposed 'to consult, advise and warn' a letter emerged in 2014 recording details of a meeting between the King and Foreign Secretary Sir Edward Grey, in which he urged his minister to 'find a reason' for going to war with Germany as the whole of Europe, including Britain, was threatened.[95]

Just as the price of silver forced a change in the silver content of coins at this time, the war also led to a shortage in gold as people began hoarding it, uncertain of what lay ahead, just as they have done since the Iron Age. Gold sovereigns and half sovereigns were soon running low, so to combat this, the Treasury, freed from the Gold Standard by the Currency and Bank Notes Act 1914, started issuing bank notes worth one pound and ten shillings just three days after the Declaration of War. They were signed by Sir John Bradbury, Permanent Secretary to the Treasury, and inevitably dubbed 'Bradburys'.

The war would prove costly; taxes would rise, international loans would be taken out, trade would slump, inflation would soar, and Britain would no longer be the economic leader of the world. The war debt would take years to pay off. A recession was on its way and there were radical changes afoot. In Ireland, following the 1916 Easter Uprising, an Irish Free State was established in 1922, with the six northern counties remaining part of the United Kingdom.

The 'Roaring Twenties' got off to a good start – at least for some. It was the time of *The Great Gatsby*, fun and games, music, and partying for the upper and some middle class. But the rumblings of unrest were beginning and unemployment was rising, particularly in the north of England. As Chancellor of the Exchequer, Winston Churchill briefly took Britain back onto the gold standard in 1925, but it was a mistake; the pound was overvalued and goods became too expensive to export, resulting in a fall in demand. He admitted later in his private letters, 'I had no special comprehension of the currency problem and therefore fell into the hands of experts...'[96] i.e. the Treasury. A General Strike broke out in 1926, a consequence of the expensive pound and a drive to reduce wages; the economic bubble the US had been enjoying burst and Wall Street crashed in 1929, followed by the Great Depression of the thirties.

---

95 *Daily Telegraph,* 26 July 2014.
96 David Lough, *No More Champagne – Churchill and His Money* (Head Zeus, 2015).

But George, who had done much to urge conciliation and had encouraged a national coalition government to tackle the growing political, economic, and international crisis, did not have long to live. Having celebrated his silver jubilee in 1935, he died early in the New Year.

13 ABDICATION TO ELIZABETH II

1936 saw three kings of Britain – George V, Edward VIII, and George VI. Edward abdicated, choosing to marry a divorced American socialite, Mrs. Wallis Simpson, so no coins were actually struck, although pattern pieces were prepared, and these can be seen in the Royal Mint Museum. The scandal surrounding the abdication forced great secrecy about these coins as indicated on the Museum's website:

> Such was the sensitivity surrounding the Abdication that for many years these patterns were locked away and not treated as part of the Museum collection; few people knew what had survived and the existence of the coins became something of a mystery even within the Royal Mint. It was not until the retirement of Sir Jack James, Deputy Master from 1957 to 1970, that a sealed cardboard box was retrieved from a safe in his office and found to contain no fewer than 49 coins of Edward VIII.[97]

The reluctant and ill-prepared Albert took the regnal name George VI (1936–1952) on becoming King with his wife, Lady Elizabeth Bowes-Lyons, at his side just as the nation faced the threat of another war with Germany.

To mark the actual coronation in 1937 commemorative crown pieces were issued. Among the new general coinage struck were five and

Edward VIII Crown pattern

---

two pound gold coins. Silver coins continued to be struck for another ten years after which they were minted in cupro-nickel.

The mood of celebration was short-lived, and when Adolf Hitler sent his troops into Poland on 1 September 1939, World War II was declared. By its end possibly as many as 85 million lives had been lost on all sides. Despite victory over Nazi Germany, it would take many years for nations to recover. In July 1944, at the Bretton Woods Conference in New Hampshire, USA, the Allies met to

> ...consult and agree on international monetary changes which affect each other. They should outlaw practices which are agreed to be harmful to world prosperity, and they should assist each other to overcome short-term exchange difficulties. [98]

It would not be until 2014 that Britain's Chancellor, George Osborne, could finally announce that the Government would pay off the outstanding £1.9 billion war loan debt on 9 March 2015.

Changes in the make-up of the British Empire began from the moment George ascended the throne. The Irish Free State removed any mention of Britain from its constitution on the day of the abdication, and the Empire itself was soon to evolve into the Commonwealth of Nations, with George becoming the first Head of the Commonwealth, and gradually the inscription IND IMP ('Emperor of India') was removed from the coinage. India achieved its independence in 1947 with the partition of the country into largely Muslim dominated Pakistan, and Hindu and Sikh India. For a short time George was formally King of both countries.

The war years triggered an ingenious plot by the Nazis to flood Britain with fake gold coins and bank notes in what was seen as a bid to break the Bank of England. The gold coins, produced by craftsmen in the concentration camps under the control of the industrialist Friedrich Schwend, were of the highest quality and many of the coins are assumed to be in circulation among

---

98 *Conference at Bretton Woods* (Pennsylvania: Book Department Army Information School, 1946).

unsuspecting collectors today.[99] Banknotes were also forged but the denominations – £5, £10, £20, and £50 – were far too high and well above a man's weekly wage, and the plot was soon uncovered.

George was a reluctant King, but a good and brave one, insisting on remaining most of the time in Buckingham Palace in central London rather than retreating to the safer confines of Windsor or the other royal estates during the war. Elizabeth in turn refused to send her children to Canada without her; she would not leave the King and the King would never leave London. So the family remained together throughout the Blitz. When a bomb fell in the grounds of the palace Elizabeth remarked, 'I'm glad we've been bombed. It makes me feel I can look the East End in the face.'

After the war the process of rebuilding and renewing became the priority. The highlight of 1951 was the staging of the Festival of Britain, described by the Festival Director, Gerald Barry, as 'a tonic to the nation,'[100] but dismissed by Winston Churchill and the opposition as 'three-dimensional Socialist propaganda'.[101] It was supposed to mark the centenary of the Great Exhibition 1851 and promote all that was good about British manufacturing and the arts. When the Labour Party was thrown out of power in the autumn of 1951 Churchill made it one of his first acts to clear London's South Bank of all the displays. What do remain in abundance are the commemorative coins some marked with the Latin inscription, '1851 By the industry of its people the State flourishes 1951'.

Unfortunately, the war years had taken their toll on George, and he failed to recover from a lung operation, dying in his sleep on 6 February 1952 while his daughter, Elizabeth, and her husband, the Duke of Edinburgh, were on tour in Kenya.

Elizabeth II (1952) was just 25 when she ascended the throne, the 40th monarch since William the Conqueror, and became the longest serving monarch, exceeding the reign of Queen Victoria, in September 2015. She has worked with 13 Prime Ministers, one

99 Peter Gill, *Operation Midas* (Peter Gill, 2014).
100 Public Information Films
101 BBC

of them, Tony Blair, was the first Prime Minister to have been born during a monarch's reign. The Queen is head of state of 16 different nations within the Commonwealth, a remarkable fact when we look back to the earliest days of the country when kings were fighting among themselves for just a corner of these islands. On 13 October 2016 she became the longest serving monarch in the world upon the death of King Bhumibol of Thailand.

Politically, the most significant change in Britain's status with regard to its nearest neighbours in Europe was the decision in 1973 to join the trading bloc, the European Economic Community – the Common Market – having twice been rejected in 1963 and 1967 by France as President Charles de Gaulle doubted the political enthusiasm of the UK. He may have been right. When in the years ahead, in 1999, Europe decided to adopt a common currency, the Euro, Britain chose to remain with sterling. The Euro may be the second most traded currency in the world after the American dollar, but Britain was having none of it, and in 2016 it was not even certain if it wanted to remain part of what had developed into much more than a trading bloc, the European Union, as strenuous efforts were made to renegotiate the terms of membership prior to a referendum on whether to stay or leave the club. In the end on 23 June 2016 the country decided after a bitter campaign that the terms on offer were not good enough and voted to leave the EU, causing political and economic upheaval not only in the UK but affecting markets worldwide as people and business digested what it meant to have a European Union without Britain for the first time in more than 40 years. The Trafalgar Square 2016 £100 fine silver coin depicting a proud British lion beneath Nelson's Column issued at the time seemed like a defiant roar of independence.

Trafalgar Square £100

Inevitably, with the length of Elizabeth's reign, there have been gradual changes to the images of her which appear on the coin; the latest design – the 5th – being unveiled on 2 March 2015. The first portrait in 1953, showing the young queen with a laurel wreath in her hair, was designed by the sculptor Mary Gillick. Unlike the reigns of old when 'recycling' the coinage was a convenient way of raising additional funds for the Treasury, today all coins remain in use until they simply wear out; there are currently some 29 billion coins in general circulation, ranging from one penny to the two pound coin which was introduced in 1994 to mark the 300th anniversary of the Bank of England.

The most significant development in coinage during Elizabeth's long reign was undoubtedly the switch to decimalisation on 15 February 1971 – fondly known as D-Day, although the historical reference is unfortunate. That day saw the end of 12 pence to the shilling, the shilling itself and 20 shillings, or 240 pennies, to the pound, valuations which had stood since the 16th century. Out went the farthing – still common currency into the 1960s when some will remember buying a loaf of bread for 11d and three farthings – and the halfpenny, the 'old' penny and the much loved threepence – 'thru'penny bit'. In their place came 100 New Pence to the pound.

It was a gradual change, beginning in 1968 with the introduction of 5 New Pence worth a shilling and 10 New Pence worth a florin. There was resistance at first, with some thinking the new money would never be accepted, until finally decimalisation was completed in 1971. One of the obstacles was the availability of loose change for coin-operated vending machines, so the popular 'old' sixpence continued to be legal tender until 1980. The inscription 'New Penny' was dropped from coins in 1982 as it was felt they were no longer 'new'.

One innovation was the two pound bimetallic coin which was the first such coin since copper plugs were used in tin farthings in the late seventeenth century to discourage forgeries.

Throughout Elizabeth's reign commemorative coins have been struck to mark important events such as her Silver and Diamond Jubilees and her children's weddings. They have also been minted on birthdays, such as in 2013 to celebrate the birth of Prince George and in 2015 the birth of Princess Charlotte to the Duke and Duchess of Cambridge, and, of course, a £20 coin was produced marking the occasion of Elizabeth becoming the longest serving monarch in September 2015, and then for those with a little extra money a £50 commemorative coin the following December.

In modern times coins are still being minted to make a point it would seem. In 1982, the Falklands War broke out between Britain and Argentina in the South Atlantic over long-standing claims of sovereignty over the islands. The war was triggered when 50 Argentines, posing as scrap metal merchants, landed on South Georgia and raised the Argentinian flag. On 2 April a larger invasion force from Argentina captured the Falkland Islands before they were retaken in June. Argentina still claims the islands (Las Malvinas) in their formal constitution, while South Georgia is known in Britain as a British Overseas Territory. In 2015, a new £2 coin depicting Elizabeth on the obverse and the islands on the reverse was struck marking the 240th anniversary of the discovery of South Georgia by Captain James Cook, who called it the Isle of George for King George III. It may be just a coin, but its message is clear.

In February 2015 the image of Britannia returned to a coin for the first time since 2008, this time on a £2 piece. Perhaps not a long break, but the Prime Minister, David Cameron, chose to underline its significance when he visited the Royal Mint, saying that Britannia was an 'enduring symbol of national identity'.[102] Britain, along

£2 Britannia

102 *Daily Telegraph,* (28 February 2015).

with other countries, felt under threat: post-9/11, when planes were hijacked and two flown into the twin towers of the World Trade Centre in New York, no city or innocent pastime seemed immune from attack, whether they were commuters travelling to work on the underground, marathon runners raising money for charities, tourists flying home from holiday, or people just enjoying some music and a drink in the evening. Cameron was driving home his firm belief in the importance of being British, standing united against all threats; just symbolic defiance on a coin perhaps, but defiance nonetheless. Little did the Prime Minister know that that very feeling of British-ness would cost him his job in June 2016 when the country rejected his plea to stay in the European Union by 52–48% in the referendum and he felt obliged to resign.

Nor did we want to forget past battles and victories. In October 2015 a £5 coin was struck to mark the 600th anniversary of the Battle of Agincourt between England and France. The designer, Glyn Davies, said he wanted to capture the mayhem when English and Welsh archers overcame a superior French force. All very well, but it may not have been a particularly diplomatic way of standing shoulder to shoulder with our European allies across the Channel.

Agincourt £5

However, commemorative coins, which are struck in their thousands, rarely hold even their face value and amount to nothing more than souvenirs, albeit tragic ones, like the coin struck to mark the wedding of Prince Charles and Lady Diana Spencer, whose marriage ended in divorce, and a year after that, the death of Princess Diana in a car accident in Paris.

Coins will continue to be minted and continue to tell their own stories, and be used to mark moments in history or underscore claims of territory and rights. It may be the monarch's face on the coin, but it is the politicians at work. They are symbols of authority as well as being used every day for mundane purchases. We barely give them a second glance as we do our shopping, certainly never read the inscriptions or consider how they have evolved, but they have been the one constant for more than 2,500 years, quietly recording our history, passing from hand to hand, just awaiting the next twist and turn. Today we seem to be trying to do without hard currency, electronically managing our finances, magically transferring billions of pounds every day in the money markets, or even just flashing our cards to pay for our daily shopping needs, but there have been moments, as we have seen, when coins have fallen out of favour only to return. We will always need something to commemorate a great occasion or mark a victory; we did it in the 1st century and we are still doing it in the 21st century. Money will go on talking.

Elizabeth II – Longest Reign

BY THE SAME AUTHOR

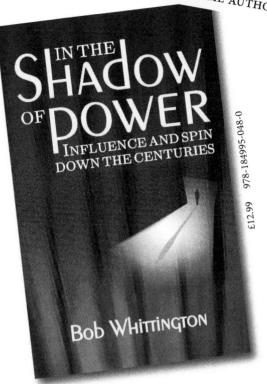

'... an interesting study of power politics among people striving
for the top table through the grisly poles of military power, wealth
and religion. ...keeps the reader absorbed as if he is reading a
novel that is a blending of adventure, intrigue and romance.
Historical facts of anecdotes further enhance the value of the
book to a discerning reader'. *India Link International*

'...a fascinating book...tells the story of many advisors and spin doctors
down the ages who assisted the good and the downright evil. It goes far,
far back, to Henry VIII and beyond, when Cardinal Thomas Wolsey
was that era's equivalent of today's immaculate gents ducking and
diving in and out the doors of Downing Street.' *The Weekly News*

www.whittlespublishing.com